Family Medical Guide

to Health & Fitness

Your best defense against sickness and disease.

The three-volume *Family Medical Guide to Health and Fitness* is a current and invaluable resource for your family's health. It covers:

- Diagnostic charts for health problems.
- How exercise and good nutrition can add years to your life.
- What to do in an emergency.
- Nutritional problems and eating disorders.
- Danger signals for cancer and heart disease.
- Easily understood descriptions of how the body works.

This home medical encyclopedia may be the best investment for the future you've ever made.

REMOVE CARD FROM POCKET AND MAIL TODAY!

FAMILY MEDICAL GUIDE

to Health & Fitness

Volume 1

Lifestyle

Volume 1

Lifestyle

FAMILY MEDICAL GUIDE

to Health & Fitness

in three volumes, illustrated

Mervyn G. Hardinge, M.D., Dr.P.H., Ph.D.
Harold Shryock, M.A., M.D.

In collaboration with 28 leading medical specialists

Published jointly by

Pacific Press Publishing Association
Boise, ID 83707
Oshawa, Ontario, Canada

Review and Herald Publishing Association
Washington, D.C. 20039-0555
Hagerstown, MD 21740

PHOTOS AND ILLUSTRATIONS

Credits for illustrations used in Volume 1 of Family Medical Guide:

Page 16 by Loma Linda University Medical Center.
Page 30 by National Aeronautics and Space Administration.
Pages 62, 63, 64, 257, 261, 267, 269, 308 by Healthstyle Productions, Inc.
Pages 20, 22, 33, 57, 58, 65, 67, 109, 118, 128, 256, 264, 322, 328, 332, 344, 345 by Duane Tank/Betty Blue.
Pages 38, 83, 112, 125, 284, 342 by Duane Tank.
Page 68 by George Deree.
Page ii, xviii, 86, 227, 340 by Betty Blue.
Page 98 by Ed Guthero.
Page 106 by Duane Tank/Ed Guthero.
Pages 106, 230 by United Press International.
Page 115 by Vic Moores.
Page 163, 190F by Stan Sinclair.

Please Note: Although the information contained in *The Family Medical Guide* is based on accurate, reliable medical knowledge, it is designed to be of a general nature and for informational purposes only. *The Family Medical Guide* is not intended to be used for self-diagnosis of medical problems nor to determine treatment apart from your physician. Always consult your physician when medical attention is indicated.

Edited by Marvin Moore
Designed by Ira Lee
Cover photo by Duane Tank and Betty Blue
Inside art by Kim Justinen
Typeset in 11/13 Century Old Style

Copyright © 1991 by
Pacific Press Publishing Association
Printed in United States of America
All Rights Reserved
Revised Edition 1994

Library of Congress Catalog Number: 90-60852

ISBN 0-8163-0813-6: Volume 1
ISBN 0-8163-0926-4: Volumes 1-3

94 95 96 97 98 ● 6 5 4 3 2

Contents

Section 4—Things to avoid

Section 5—Understanding medications

Volume 2—Family health and general diseases

Section 1—The stages of life

Section 2—Medical care at home

Section 3—General diseases

Volume 3—The systems of the body and their disorders

Section 1—The cardiovascular and lymphatic systems and their disorders

Section 2—The digestive and respiratory systems and their disorders

Section 3—The skeletal and cutaneous systems and their disorders

Section 4—The endocrine and nervous systems and their disorders

Section 5—The reproductive and urinary systems and their disorders

Section 6—The sense organs and their disorders

Collaborating specialists

The authors wish to thank the specialists in the various fields of medicine and related disciplines who assisted as consultants in the preparation of the *Family Medical Guide*. Most of them are faculty members or former faculty members at Loma Linda University in Loma Linda, California. The schools in which they teach are designated with abbreviations. A key to these abbreviations is given at the end of the list of consultants.

Elvin Adams, M.D., M.P.H. Practicing physician (internal medicine), Fort Worth, Texas; former medical director, U.S. Office of Smoking and Health, U.S.P.H.S.

Charles Anderson, M.D., L.F.A.P.A. Life Fellow, American Psychiatric Association

Jeanne D. Andrews, M.D. Associate Professor of Pediatrics, SM

James Crawford, D.D.S., M.P.H. Professor of Preventive and Community Dentistry, SD

Clarence W. Dail, M.D. Professor Emeritus of Medicine (physical medicine and rehabilitation), SM

Harvey Elder, M.D. Professor of Medicine (infectious disease, hospital epidemiology), SM

Glenn L. Foster, M.D. Professor of Medicine (cardiology), SM

Henry L. Hadley, M.D. Professor of Urology, SM

Richard H. Hart, M.D., Dr.P.H. Professor of Preventive Medicine, SM

Guy M. Hunt, M.D., M.S. Professor of Medicine (neurology and anatomy), SM

N. Eric Johnson, M.D. Assistant Professor of Emergency Medicine, SM

Timothy T. K. Jung, M.D., Ph.D. Associate Professor of Surgery (otolaryngology), SM

Edwin H. Krick, M.D., M.P.H. Associate Professor of Medicine (immunology), SM

Eva Miller, M.S. Associate Professor of Community Health Nursing, SN

Robert Mitchell, M.D. Professor of Medicine (gastroenterology), SM

James Munson, M.D. Assistant Clinical Professor of Pediatrics (allergy), SM

J. Lamont Murdoch, M.D. Professor of Medicine (endocrinology), SM

Dave Nieman, Dr.H.Sc. Associate Professor, Department of Health, Leisure, and Exercise, Appalachian State University, Boone, North Carolina

Robert L. Nutter, Ph.D. Professor of Microbiology (virology and cancer), SM (retired)

U. D. Register, Ph.D. Professor of Nutrition, School of Public Health, SPH
Elmer P. Sakala, M.D. Professor of Gynecology and Obstetrics, SM
Gordon Thompson, M.D. Assistant Professor of Medicine (chest), SM
Bernard Tilton, M.D., Ph.D. Professor of Pharmacology, SM
Robert Torrey, M.D. Assistant Professor of Urology, SM
Ingrid Trenkle, M.D. Practicing physician (dermatology), Redlands, California
Edward D. Wagner, Ph.D. Professor of Microbiology (parasitology), SM
Arnold V. Wallenkampf, Ph.D. Formerly Professor of Religion, SR
George Wiesseman, M.D. Associate Professor of Orthopedic Surgery, SM
Raymond O. West, M.D. Professor of Family Medicine, SM (retired)
Ernest Zane, M.D. Associate Professor of Ophthalmology, SM (retired)

SD = School of Dentistry
SM = School of Medicine
SN = School of Nursing
SPH = School of Public Health
SR = School of Religion

Introduction to the Family Medical Guide

The *Family Medical Guide to Health and Fitness* is the most recent in a long line of books about health published by Pacific Press. The first book, *Colds, the Science of Taking Them* (was that advice on how to catch a cold?) by Dr. Hermann Portsch, was published in 1890—exactly 100 years from the copyright date on the *Family Medical Guide*. Our first book of general medical advice for the home was published eleven years later in 1901—the *Family Medical Book* by Melinda Goldson. We have continued publishing family medical guides from that time to the present.

Three principles have dominated each of these books. First is Pacific Press's commitment to bring to your home the most up-to-date medical advice available at the time of publication. Second is our belief that prevention is even more important than cure. And third is our conviction that there is a close relationship between physical and spiritual health.

Each of these principles is evident in the *Family Medical Guide*. From the first page of volume 1 to the last page of volume 3, these books contain the most modern advice available in the field of medicine. Our commitment to preventing disease wherever possible is evident in the fact that the entire first volume is about how to live a healthful lifestyle.

An entire section in volume 1 deals with spiritual and emotional health. However, our conviction that physical and spiritual health are closely united goes far beyond the mere inclusion of a chapter here or a section there on spiritual health. We believe that a healthy body contributes to a healthy mind and a healthy spirit. Nobody can be spiritually strong who is physically run-down. It is impossible for a person to have a close personal relationship with God and at the same time abuse his body with alcohol, tobacco, and narcotics or weaken it through lack of rest or poor nutrition. Sickness dulls the senses and makes it much more difficult for God to reach our minds. Therefore we should avoid disease insofar as possible and recover our health as quickly as possible when we do get sick.

From this you can see that the whole purpose of the *Family Medical Guide* is not only to help you have a strong, healthy body but also to help you develop a strong mind and a closer relationship with your Creator.

We hope that the *Family Medical Guide* will become your key to a long and happy life.

How to use the Family Medical Guide

The *Family Medical Guide to Health and Fitness* is one of your most valuable tools for preserving your health and for recovering when you get sick. However, like any tool, it will only work for you when you use it. The more you use it, the more it will do for you. The following suggestions will help you to get the most out of your *Family Medical Guide.*

General organization

We recommend that you begin by turning to the table of contents at the beginning of this volume (or any of the volumes, since each one lists the contents of all of them). Familiarize yourself with the general structure of the *Family Medical Guide.* Discover for yourself how it is organized, so that you can more quickly pick up the right volume and turn to just the right place when you have a question or need help with a problem.

Near the end of volume 1 you will find a glossary of medical and health terms that will help you understand what the authors mean when they use words you are unfamiliar with. At the end of each volume is an index, which, like the table of contents, covers the entire three-volume series. It doesn't matter which volume you pick up; the index will direct you to the information you need in all three volumes.

Sometimes one health problem is related to another. Rather than waste valuable space repeating the information about a particular condition each time it is mentioned, where they felt it important to do so, the authors and the publishers have provided cross-references that will direct you quickly to the additional information you need.

The three volumes are paged consecutively. That is, volume 2 picks up where volume 1 leaves off, and 3 picks up where 2 leaves off. The page numbers within each volume are listed on the spine, making it easy for you to know exactly which volume to choose when looking for a particular item by page number.

Volume 2 includes a whole section on emergency medicine for the home. These pages have a red border that you can see when the book is closed, making it easy for you to turn quickly to that section when you need help fast. The first page of the emergency section includes an index of life-threatening health problems that will help you to avoid wasting valuable time finding help.

Preventing illness

The *Family Medical Guide* is unique. It is one of the few health books (or sets of books) on the market today that combines an explanation of disease (and recovery from disease) with how to prevent disease in the first place. There are lots of books on prevention and lots of books on disease and cure, but few that bring everything together.

We recommend that you read through volume 1, which explains how to have a healthy lifestyle. Keep a pen or pencil handy as you read, and make notes about the points you come across that will help you to be more healthy. (You may be surprised at how much you learn about maintaining your health that you didn't know about.) If you put the page number beside each note as you write, you can quickly refer to the discussion later, when you may have forgotten all the details.

The nutritional charts in volume 1 are obviously not for reading the way you'll read the rest of the book. They are reference material. We recommend that you use these charts to analyze your diet (see page 129). Not that you will analyze every meal the rest of your life! Do it for just one week. If you find that your diet is out of balance in certain ways, use the charts to help you know which foods will help you to improve. Once you get used to using them, you'll find yourself turning frequently to the nutrition charts for information.

Volume 1 also includes many recipes to help you prepare nutritious food that tastes good. The nutritional analysis with each recipe will help you to evaluate its contribution to your overall diet. Again, the idea is not to check the nutritional content of every recipe you or the cook in your family prepares the rest of your life. But taking the time for a few weeks to check the nutritional content of each recipe you prepare will give you a "feel" for the nutritional content of various foods. Once you

get this "feel," you will be able to prepare nutritious meals almost by instinct.

Near the end of volume 1 you will find several pages of drug charts that will help you to learn more about the dangerous street drugs so popular in the United States and other parts of the world today. If you use illicit drugs, you need to look up the one (or ones) you take to find out the problems it can cause. If you know someone else who uses drugs, these charts can help you know how to talk to him or her about the problem.

Recovery from illness

Throughout all three volumes you will find simple descriptions of the major health problems that people in the United States are likely to encounter, and the majority of problems that people in other parts of the world are likely to encounter as well. But how can you find the information you need without looking through all three volumes? The *Family Medical Guide* provides three ways to find the information you need about a specific illness.

The first thing you should do when you or someone you know gets sick is to turn to the chapter, "Common problems and symptoms," in volume 2 and look for the symptom that seems to be most characteristic of that illness. The symptoms are listed alphabetically. Each item describes that symptom briefly and tells you where to turn elsewhere in the three volumes for additional information.

Another excellent guide when you or someone you know gets sick is the flowcharts in the chapter "Ready diagnosis of common problems." Look for the chart that discusses one of your symptoms. Each flowchart will help you to identify which is the most probable cause of that symptom in your case, and it will alert you if the condition is a medical emergency. Where necessary, it will also give you the page number to turn to for more information about that problem or condition.

And, of course, the general index at the back of each volume will also help you to find the information you need about particular problems and illnesses.

imbalance results first in malfunction, and if not checked, leads to tissue breakdown and finally disease.

Consider, for a moment, the Apollo mission to the moon. The lunar module required elaborate support and guidance systems in order to accomplish its objective. Even the astronaut, as he walked on the surface of the moonscape, carried his support unit strapped to his back and was guided by instructions coming from the earth.

It's the same with your body. Every functional unit must have adequate support and appropriate guidance to carry out its every activity.

The following table divides the body into functional units, support systems, and guidance systems. The smallest of all functional units are the enzymes: protein molecules specifically designed to do a single chemical task. These molecules are the body's workmen. If several steps are required to complete the task, there will be a corresponding number of enzymes to accomplish each step. Such a group of enzymes is called an enzyme system.

The "factories" in which the enzymes work are located in the cells. The command center of each cell is the nucleus. Each enzyme must be supported and directed in order to fulfill its task. The raw materials and the energy to drive these enzyme factories come from the food you eat by way of your digestive system. Your blood is the body's transportation system. In the lungs oxygen is picked up, and waste carbon dioxide is expelled. Chemical wastes are carried to the kidneys to be eliminated in the urine.

All these and countless parallel activities are regulated by the hormones and guided by the nervous system.

When every functional unit is working efficiently, each within its own physiological range, and is adequately supported and appropriately guided, you have health, and your

The organization of the body		
Functional units	**Support systems**	**Guidance systems**
Enzymes	Respiration	Nervous
Cells	Circulation	Hormonal
Glands or organs	Digestion	Mechanical
	Elimination	

body is able to resist disease. But when the biological range is exceeded, that is, when there is either an excess or deficiency in a particular area, the result is imbalance, and you

The body constantly maintains a "normal" temperature by mechanisms that decrease or increase heat loss.

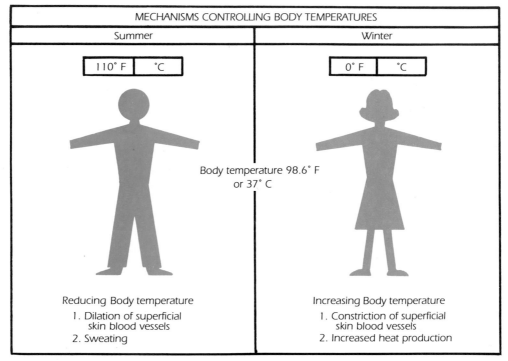

MECHANISMS CONTROLLING BODY TEMPERATURES	
Summer	Winter
110° F °C	0° F °C
Body temperature 98.6° F or 37° C	
Reducing Body temperature	Increasing Body temperature
1. Dilation of superficial skin blood vessels 2. Sweating	1. Constriction of superficial skin blood vessels 2. Increased heat production

become susceptible to disease. To illustrate this, let us consider three examples: blood pressure, body temperature, and blood sugar.

In healthy individuals blood pressure averages between 120 and 60 mm Hg (or the number of millimeters the pressure would raise a column of mercury if the other end were attached to the artery). However, if your pressure rises above 140 or 90 and remains there for long periods of time, you have high blood pressure, or "hypertension." On the other hand, if your higher level of blood pressure suddenly drops to 80 or 60 or even to 40, you have low blood pressure, or "hypotension,"

and serious problems will result.

Your body temperature is not static but varies from time to time, even during the course of a day. Early in the morning it is generally a little below 98.6°F (37°C). However, as the day goes by it rises to the normal temperature, and may exceed this level in midafternoon. However, when the temperature shoots up to 104 degrees, you are said to have a fever. On the other hand, should you be exposed to a severe cold, and should your core body temperature fall to 90°F, you would have the serious problem of "hypothermia."

The level of sugar in your blood also changes throughout the day.

After a meal your sugar level slowly rises, giving you a feeling of satisfaction. As it gradually falls to fasting levels, you begin to feel hungry. But should your blood sugar level remain far above the usual post-meal high for a prolonged period, you would face the problem of diabetes. Should your blood sugar level remain significantly below your pre-meal level, the disorder would be low blood sugar, or hypoglycemia.

So you can see that throughout your body there are normal ranges of function. Persistent deviations from these limits result in imbalance and disease. Stated another way, exceeding the upper or lower limits of your biological range causes malfunction and disease, while operating within these limits brings balance and health. Living healthfully makes each of us resistant to disease, while living unhealthfully makes us susceptible to illness.

You determine your lifestyle, and thereby control your health and your likelihood of succumbing to disease. If you have high regard for the laws that govern your body, you will have a healthful lifestyle. To the extent that you disregard these laws, to that extent your lifestyle will be unhealthful.

Whenever you allow your activities to push you above or below this physiological range, you become susceptible to illness. Inadequate rest or excessive work makes you over-fatigued. Agents of disease are ever present, resulting in the onset of colds and other infections. But often germs need not play a role. Prolonged states of anxiety and stress may also cause problems such as hypertension, stomach ulcers, and insomnia.

Your habits of life—good and bad—determine your lifestyle. The long-term effects of cigarette smoking are well known. The use of beverage alcohol may terminate in alcoholism, cirrhosis of the liver, or damage to the heart. Inactivity may make you prone to coronary heart disease and osteoporosis, while overeating can lead to obesity and adult-onset diabetes.

You are the arbiter of your future. If you disregard nature's laws, the result is likely to be disease and premature death, while a high regard to these same laws is your best assurance of a long and healthy life.

The habits of life largely determine the level of health or the degree of illness.

CHAPTER 4

Exercise

For hundreds of millions of people in various countries of the world, exercise is a necessary part of life, for hard physical labor is required to provide the essentials for survival. Only recently has it been recognized that this labor has actually protected these populations against a wide variety of degenerative diseases. For other millions, in other countries, machines now do what muscles were designed to do, and lack of exercise is exacting a staggering toll of sickness and death from diseases caused by disuse of the body and the mind. It is imperative, then, to understand just how exercise plays this important role.

Animals and their organ systems are all programmed. The lifestyles for which they were designed, which make it possible for them to live in the environment in which they exist, provide all the exercise they need to keep them in top physical condition.

While man's organ systems are also programmed, there is one notable exception. Man has been left the responsibility of using his skeletal muscles—those muscles that attach to his bones. In a healthy person, these muscles comprise some 46 percent of the body mass and function under the control of the voluntary nervous system—that is, the will. These muscles do your every bidding. They make it possible for you to scratch your nose, open your mouth, close your eyes, get dressed, feed yourself; and they transport you from place to place. You are answerable for their use.

It is a law of nature that whatever is not used weakens and deterio-

Vigorous
Exercise

Some
Exercise

No
Exercise

Only one out of every five Americans obtains adequate exercise.

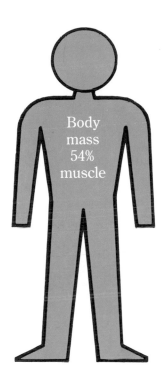

Of all the structures of the body, more than half (54 percent) of a fit person is muscle.

rates. This is true of your voluntary muscles. Failure to use or exercise them judiciously makes them weak and flabby. The bones to which they attach also weaken, losing their mineral deposits, and produce a condition known as osteoporosis. But much more depends on exercising your muscles.

Your involuntary muscles constitute 8 percent of your body mass. These are present in the walls of your stomach, intestines, urinary bladder, and blood vessels. In a somewhat modified form they also make up your heart. These involuntary muscles are not controlled by your will, but rather are preprogrammed to carry out their functions

(voluntary control of the diaphragm may be overridden). However, they are driven to more active use as you exercise your voluntary muscles. So when you fail to exercise your voluntary muscles regularly, your involuntary muscles also weaken and deteriorate.

Failure to exercise results in the weakening of those organs and systems that are formed from involuntary muscles. The only way to have a strong heart, clean, resilient blood vessels, good digestion, and adequate elimination, is to exercise.

What exercise involves

When you begin to exercise, the muscles act like furnaces. They contract, or shorten, by burning your food fuel. This uses up oxygen, and the energy produces wastes and gives off heat. A signal is sent to your heart to beat more forcefully in order to bring additional oxygen and fuel, and to carry off the wastes and heat. Your heart now puts out more blood per beat and more beats per minute. Your vessels dilate to carry the extra blood to and from the working muscles. This strengthens your heart and keeps your arteries supple.

As more blood is brought to the surface, the vessels of your skin dilate to liberate the heat, and you now begin to sweat. The evaporating moisture eliminates certain body wastes and further dissipates heat to maintain your normal temperature.

The respiratory system is signaled to provide more oxygen and eliminate more carbon dioxide, and so you breathe more rapidly and more

35

deeply. This strengthens your dia-phragm and chest muscles—the muscles of respiration.

As the intensity of exercise rises, blood flow through the muscles greatly increases.

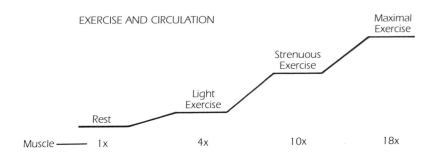

EXERCISE AND CIRCULATION

Maximal Exercise

Strenuous Exercise

Light Exercise

Rest

Muscle —— 1x 4x 10x 18x

Your body draws on its energy re-serves so the muscles you've chosen to exercise can keep going, and this sends a signal to your digestive sys-tem to provide more fuel from food. This sharpens your appetite, tones up your stomach and intestines, and encourages the elimination of waste from your colon.

The chemical wastes entering the blood must be filtered through your kidneys and washed out through your urinary system.

Your contracting muscles them-selves strengthen, placing greater pull on the bones to which they are attached. The bones, in turn, become thicker, denser, and stronger. The movement of your bones lubricates the cartilage in the joints and strengthens your ligaments.

Your brain must direct and control not only the form of physical work or exercise you are doing, but must also help to order and regulate the vast amount of activity within the organ systems of your now vigorously functioning body. The choices and decisions the brain must make give it

strength and keep it alert.

So when you exercise your volun-tary muscles, you automatically exer-cise your involuntary muscles and your brain and nervous system. Thus every structure and organ of your body is strengthened and in-vigorated.

Benefits of exercise

Following are some of the benefits that you get from vigorous exercise:

- It tones and strengthens every organ and system of your body.
- It helps relax tensions, making your sleep sounder.
- It strengthens your self-control, in-creases your mental efficiency, and enhances your feeling of well-being.
- It decreases depression and anxiety.
- It lowers emotional stress.
- It lowers blood fats (triglycerides) and increases good cholesterol HDL), thus helping to reduce your risk of coronary heart disease and stroke.

- It decreases insulin resistance, aids in the control of blood sugar levels, and is of value in the treatment of diabetes (type I and type II).
- It helps relieve constipation.
- It protects you against osteoporosis.
- It increases your endurance for both work and play.
- It lengthens your life expectancy (delays the onset of aging).

Speaking of the benefits of exercise, Doctor Paffenbarger of Stanford University says, "For each hour of physical activity, you can expect to live that hour over and live one or two hours to boot." And then he adds, "If cancer were eliminated as a cause of death, the years of life gained would be about the same" as those obtained from a regular exercise program.[1]

A few words of caution

- Before embarking on your personal exercise program, ask your doctor to give you a physical examination. This is especially important if you have not exercised for a long time, have any cardiovascular problem, have high blood pressure, are a diabetic, are taking a medication, or are under the care of a physician for some illness. Also ask your doctor if there are any precautions you should take.
- Do the following warm-up exercises before you start to exercise: bend the joints of your arms and legs back and forth (flexion and extension) and stretch your back, arms, and legs. Do these exercises slowly, without any jerky or thrusting movements. Stretch till you begin to feel some tension. Hold for about fifteen seconds, and then relax.
- Do not try to become fit overnight. Your fitness program should start slowly and gradually increase in intensity. Remember, you did not become "unfit" in a day.
- Drink plenty of water before, during, and after exercising. Dehydration will cause you to feel fatigued (see pages 80, 963) and might bring on a headache or cause muscle cramps.

Frequency
Intensity
Time

A good exercise program is built on how often (frequency), how vigorous (intensity), and how long (time) one exercises, summarized in the acronym FIT.

How much exercise

The acronym **FIT** beautifully embodies the ingredients of a good exercise program:

- **F**—frequency determines how often you should exercise. Research has shown that exercising three to five times each week is all that is necessary.

- **I**—intensity has to do with how hard or vigorously you exercise. Exercises may be mild, moderate, or strenuous.

- **T**—time signifies how long you exercise. Depending on your circumstances, you may exercise anywhere from a few minutes to several hours each day. You need to put in at least thirty minutes each time you exercise. If you choose an exercise of low intensity, you will have to exercise longer. Within limits, a high intensity exercise can be done for a shorter time. Any exercise program should be tailored to your needs.

- **FIT,** then, means that you should exercise three to five times each week, and the exercise should be moderate to strenuous, lasting between twenty and thirty minutes each session.

Aerobic exercise

Aerobic is a Greek word that means "air." Aerobic exercises are those that are vigorous enough to increase your body's demand for oxygen (air) and that strengthen both your heart and lungs by forcing them to work harder. Although all forms of exercise have certain common benefits, different kinds of exercise emphasize different aspects of fitness. These include endurance, flexibility, strength, agility, coordination, and physical dexterity. The chart on the next page classifies a number of common exercises according to whether they are light, moderate, strenuous, or extremely vigorous. You can easily see that the same exercise may fall into several categories.

Walking, for example, is the easiest, cheapest, and safest type of exercise. If you have not been in the habit of exercising and wish to start a fitness program, you can begin by walking slowly for a short distance each day. As your strength increases, you can walk fairly briskly for a longer distance. Your walking has now become a moderate form of exercise. Striding can make it a vigorous activity.

In order to build fitness you should exercise vigorously for at least thirty minutes three times a week or more.

Intensity of exercises			
Light	**Moderate**	**Heavy**	**Very heavy**
Walking	Walking briskly	Climbing hills	Backpacking
		Running (moderate)	Running (vigorous)
Cycling (leisure)	Cycling (moderate)		Cycling (racing)
		Swimming (slow)	Swimming (fast)
Gardening (easy)	Hoeing	Gardening (vigorous)	
Carpentry	Golfing	Aerobic dancing	Cross-country skiing

Your exercise program

How can you determine how much you should exercise? The following simple formula is based on the condition of your heart. Assume that you are fifty years old. Now subtract your age from 220. The result is 170. Find 75 percent of 170 (0.75 x 170), which comes to 128. If you are fifty years old, your target heart rate (number of beats per minutes) or training zone is 128, plus or minus 5.

To determine your pulse rate you need a watch with a second hand. Count your pulse at your wrist or neck (see page 573). By counting for ten seconds and multiplying by six,

you will know your heart rate per minute.

After a short warm-up period (five to ten minutes), start your exercise. Let's say it's walking. Stop every five or ten minutes and check your heart rate. If it is over 133 you are exercising too much, so slow down; if it is under 123 you are exercising too little, so speed up. Work within your

PERFORMANCE	
Physically Unfit	**Physically Fit**
Efficiency decreased	Efficiency increased
More energy needed	Less energy needed
More waste	Less waste
Early fatigue	Delayed fatigue
Prolonged recovery	Rapid recovery

tolerance. If you get sore, stiff muscles, you have overdone it, so ease up. Just be consistent, and in time you will reach your goal of fitness.

As you become fit, you will find it more and more difficult to reach your target heart rate. That is what you want. It shows that the blood your weak, flabby heart had been pumping in 128 beats a minute, your conditioned heart can now pump in 115 or even 100 beats a minute. Now you can increase either the rate or the distance you walk. As you become physically fit, you will enjoy a feeling of well-being that is worth all your effort.

Choosing the best exercise

Some people do not enjoy exercise. If you are one of these, you will have

A REGULAR EXERCISE PROGRAM

● Improves circulation

● Improves well-being

● Decreases anxiety

● Decreases depression

● Increases mental efficiency

● Lengthens life

to use mental discipline and learn to get pleasure from your exercise. Preliminary research done by one of the authors found that those who enjoyed their exercise reduced their blood cholesterol levels significantly. Those who did not, neither lowered nor raised their levels.

When **walking** or **striding,** one of your feet will be in contact with the ground at all times, so that you gently transfer your body weight from one foot to the other. When you **jog** (a slow run) or **run,** both feet are momentarily in the air, so that when your foot strikes the ground, it makes an impact. When this impact is on a hard surface such as concrete, black-top, or a gym floor, your joints may in time suffer injury, or you may develop shin splints (see page 941). A good pair of shoes will decrease your likelihood of developing impact injuries, but better still, choose an exercise that is adapted to your specific needs and abilities.

If you cannot participate in outdoor exercise, develop an exercise program in your home. Some people enjoy simple calisthenics. Others like running in place. You may wish to get a trampoline, an exercise bicycle, or a rowing machine. Your local YMCA or YWCA may have programs to offer. During the summer you may wish to swim. Swimming is an excellent exercise for those who have arthritis, since swimming does not bring weight to bear on the joints, and the warm water tends to relax tense muscles. Remember, any form of exercise is better than no exercise at all.

The key to well-being

While it is unwise to link good health to any single health practice, if we were to do so, exercise would stand at the top of the list. The best diet in the world will not be of great value if your body furnaces are smoldering and the flues are clogged. A weak heart, sluggish circulation, flabby muscles, demineralized bones, shallow respiration, poor digestion, and faulty elimination—all these go along with physical inactivity. So why not resolve to have an exercise program suited to your needs—and start today.

Exercise and high altitude[2]

With the increased interest in outdoor exercise in the United States and other western countries, large numbers of people are taking up the sports of mountain climbing in the summer months and skiing during the winter season. Most of these hikers and skiers live near or at sea level but are moved rapidly to high altitudes by car, bus, or plane. With no opportunity to acclimatize, they plunge into activities that require strenuous physical exertion. This abrupt exposure to high altitudes results in an increased incidence of high altitude illness.

Those who stay in lodges below 7,000 feet rarely develop problems. Studies indicate that **altitude illness** begins at about 8,000 feet (2,440 m), and the incidence of mountain sickness and pulmonary edema are more often encountered at 9,000 feet. At 8,000 feet the blood (arterial) oxygen level is 89 percent, and it drops to 77 percent at 14,000 feet (4,270 m). Those reaching **high altitudes** (beyond 14,000 feet), even for short periods, show a still higher incidence of severe medical problems.

The medical problems are even more severe from abrupt ascent to **very high altitudes,** between 14,000 and 18,000 feet (4,270-5,490 m). **Extremely high altitudes** are those above 18,000 feet, reaching up to the world's highest peak, Mount Everest, at 29,028 feet (8,848 m). Most people who are not acclimatized fail to reach these levels. Experience has shown that the altitude at which a person sleeps is more important in determining whether altitude illness will occur than the altitudes reached during a day of climbing or skiing. The saying "sleep low and climb high" appears to have physiologic validity.

Physiologic changes at high altitude

Some of the changes seen at high altitude are due to the body's efforts to compensate for a reduced concentration of oxygen. Others result from an inability to adapt, and are indicators of impending illness. Among the changes commonly observed are:

- decrease in the concentration of blood (arterial) oxygen
- increase in the depth and rate of breathing

- increased alkalinity of the blood (respiratory alkalosis) due to rapid breathing and an excessive loss of carbon dioxide
- increased concentration of the blood due to shifts in body water
- increase in the number of red blood cells, resulting from concentration of the blood and an increase in the production of red blood cells
- altered heart rate (the heart generally beats faster but less efficiently)

The overall effect is a loss in physical performance, and the capacity to exercise is decreased.

Acclimatization

A person who is not acclimated to high altitude suffers from a variety of symptoms, including headache, lassitude, weakness, dizziness, and fatigue. His ability to perform work is greatly diminished. The body makes every effort to adapt to the lower level of oxygen. This adaptation is known as acclimatization and takes hours, days, weeks, or months, depending on the altitude and the individual. The major means by which this is accomplished include:

- increased breathing, both depth and rate
- an increase in the number of red blood cells, providing more hemoglobin to carry oxygen
- increased ability of the lungs to pick up oxygen
- increased number of capillaries in the tissues so oxygen can more readily reach the tissue cells

- increased use of oxygen by the tissue cells due to enzyme changes within the cells

The degree of acclimatization can be observed by the disappearance of unpleasant symptoms and an increase in work performance.

Acclimatization is accomplished by either staging or graded ascent. **Staging** involves staying at one or more intermediate altitudes for two to four days at a time. **Graded ascent** is a gradual daily increase in altitude over a period of days or weeks. Experience suggests that above 14,000 feet, a 1,000-foot (305 m) gain in altitude each day is sufficient, and that a day of rest every other day is beneficial.

Natural acclimatization

Natives born and raised in the Himalayas and in the Andes at altitudes above 13,000 feet (3,965 m) tend to develop large chests (barrel) and relatively smaller bodies so that the oxygen delivered to the tissues is greatly increased. The other characteristics of acclimatization (discussed above) are also naturally present. These natives can live and work indefinitely at very high altitudes, compared with those who grow up at lower altitudes and attempt to acclimatize. The latter should descend to lower latitudes (below 8,000 feet) at least once a year for three to four weeks at a time in order to maintain their health.

Acute mountain sickness

Most individuals develop acute mountain sickness if they are abruptly taken to 12,000 feet (3,660 m) or higher. The most common symptoms include a severe throbbing headache that increases with exercise, feelings of illness, tiredness, weakness, and dizziness. Loss of appetite is typical, and is associated with nausea and often vomiting. Sleep is disturbed. The lips may be blue, there may be a dry cough, and walking may be difficult. The intensity of mountain sickness varies from (1) mild, involving little interference with activity, to (2) moderately severe, where activity is difficult, to (3) severe, where the individual is incapacitated. Disturbed mental functions and lapses of consciousness generally indicate pulmonary or cerebral edema.

Depending on the individual and the altitude, the symptoms usually subside in two to seven days. When the condition warrants it, rest in bed, fluids, a light diet, and medication to relieve the headache are helpful. Breathing pure oxygen may also provide relief. Your physician may prescribe a drug called Acetazolamide to relieve symptoms, and sometimes as a preventive. When the condition is severe (pulmonary and cerebral edema), the sufferer should be promptly taken to lower altitudes.

Exercise at low altitudes does not protect against the onset of acute mountain sickness, but appropriate acclimatization usually does.

Subacute mountain sickness

Some individuals fail to compensate for the high altitude in which they live, and the symptoms of acute mountain sickness persist for months. The condition is seen in those who have moved from sea level to employment at 12,000 feet (3,660 m) and above. Loss of appetite with marked weight loss, inability to sleep well, constant fatigue and sleepiness, together with slowing of mental processes and emotional swings, are frequently observed. The problem resolves on descending to lower altitudes.

Chronic mountain sickness

This problem develops in a few individuals after relatively prolonged residence (months to years) at altitudes above 10,000 feet (3,050 m). Weakness, difficulty in breathing, fatigue, and the inability to think clearly gradually increase. The number of red blood cells is greatly increased. The right side of the heart enlarges in an effort to circulate the blood through the lungs, and the heart may ultimately fail. The oxygen level in the tissues drops, and death may occur unless the person is taken to lower altitudes, where recovery is usually complete. It is unwise for such persons to return to high altitudes, as the problem usually recurs.

High altitude pulmonary edema

Pulmonary edema, as the name implies, is the accumulation of fluid in the lungs, with a resulting deficiency of available oxygen to the brain and other body organs. It is usually seen in those who rapidly ascend to altitudes of 8,000 feet (2,440 m) or higher, and who engage in strenuous physical activity (skiing, climbing, etc.). Difficult breathing, coughing, and extreme fatigue are common. Loss of appetite with nausea and vomiting may also occur. An inability to think clearly, with delirium and hallucinations, may be followed by unconsciousness and coma.

Pulmonary edema should be suspected if other conditions do not clearly rule it out. An accelerated resting heart rate, rapid breathing, and fluid in the lungs are clear signs. The victim should be removed to a low altitude immediately. Postponing the descent because of bad weather, to wait for daylight, or for the arrival of a rescue team may prove fatal. If it is available, oxygen should be given by face mask. If diagnosed early, and if the sufferer is promptly taken to a lower altitude, rest alone may be sufficient for recovery. Otherwise hospitalization is essential.

High altitude cerebral edema

Persons who ascend rapidly to altitudes over 12,000 (3,660 m) are subject to this problem, which manifests itself in about 10 days. It is more commonly seen in those suffering from pulmonary edema. A reduced level of oxygen in the brain tissues apears to contribute to the outflow of fluid, with resulting compression of the brain itself. The common symptoms include headache, weakness, vomiting, inability to coordinate movements, irrational behavior, hemorrages into the retina, coma, and death.

Recognition of the problem, with rapid descent to lower altitudes and giving adequate oxygen, are the best remedies. The victim should be kept in a sitting position, as this tends to lower pressure within the brain. To prevent the condition, acclimatization procedures as discussed under acute mountain sickness should be employed.

Retinal hemorrhages

These result from increased pressure in the vessels of the eye, which is caused by insufficient oxygen in the tissues. They are commonly seen at altitudes above 14,000 feet (4,270 m), and are present in almost all those ascending above 20,000 (6,100 m). The hemorrhages generally disappear as soon as the sufferer returns to a lower altitude.

1. "Extra Years for Extra Effort," *Time,* March 17, 1986, p. 66.

2 The authors have drawn heavily from an excellent article, "High Altitude Medical Problems," which appeared in "Current Topics in Medicine," *Scientific America Medicine,* 1990, chapter IX, pp. 1-11.

CHAPTER 5

Fatigue

In the biological world any functional unit, from a single enzyme to a complex system like the brain, when activated, functions at maximum efficiency. This efficiency is reduced only if there exists an excess or a deficiency of some substance in the organism's environment, or if there is interference from some outside source. However, even though an organism functions perfectly, if it functions continually, it will eventually become fatigued.

As a functional unit becomes fatigued, its ability to perform its task is reduced, and it continues to decline as fatigue increases. Thus fatigue may actually be a protective mechanism, preventing the irreversible damage that might result from continual activity.

The brain is made up of specialized cells, and like the specialized cells of other organs, it also becomes fatigued with continued use. Thus you can become both physically and mentally fatigued. Fatigue is brought about by long hours of physical work, long hours of mental work, and loss of sleep. Fatigue develops from a lack of physical or mental rest, and one is usually more dominant than the other.

When you become **physically fatigued** through prolonged muscular activity, your muscles become relaxed and their tone diminished. This occurs when you work in the garden or go for a swim or play some game. This is called **hypotonic fatigue.**

But with increasing **mental fatigue** the capacity to work is also diminished, but instead of becoming relaxed you become tense and tired. You experience this when you have worked long hours in the office and everything seems to have gone wrong. This is known as **hypertonic fatigue.**

Modern society makes heavy demands on body and mind. The pace of life is fast, and the pressure of work and activity is high. In this environment you, like those around you, tax yourself to the breaking point. You never take time to really rest and recuperate. You, like millions of others, live in a state of chronic fatigue.

A. HYPOTONIC (RELAXED) FATIGUE

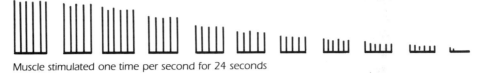

Muscle stimulated one time per second for 24 seconds

B. HYPERTONIC (TENSION) FATIGUE

Muscle stimulated 4 times per second for 2 minutes

The contractions of the thigh muscles of a frog stimulated at varying rates. Recovery time between contractions was longer in A than in B, showing relaxed and tensed fatigue respectively.

Characteristics of fatigue

Whether you are suffering from physical or mental fatigue, performance is reduced. Some of the common characteristics of fatigue are outlined in the table below. When you are tired you perform like a beginner or someone who is learning to do a task. Think of the time you were trying to learn to ride a bicycle or to swim. You were inefficient, and it took you a dis-

proportionate amount of effort. You consumed more energy. This consumption of extra energy produced more waste, increasing the workload of your body.

When you are inadequately rested, you will become tired more rapidly and it will take longer for you to recover. A common example is when you are carrying a heavy suitcase and are late for an appointment. You change your suitcase from one hand

Performance	
Fatigued	**Rested**
Efficiency decreased	Efficiency increased
More energy needed	Less energy needed
More waste	Less waste
Early fatigue	Delayed fatigue
Prolonged recover	Rapid recovery

her first child before age twenty-five has a lower risk of breast cancer than does the woman who has her first child after age thirty-five.

However, marriage seems to have just the opposite effect in cancer of the cervix. Among girls married in their teens, or who first experience sexual intercourse in their early

they are at increased risk (see predisposing factors and lifestyle factors on the preceding pages) should be alert to the telltale signs and symptoms that indicate the possible presence of a cancer. For example, smokers are in a high risk category, not only for cancer of the lung (90 percent of all lung cancers), but for

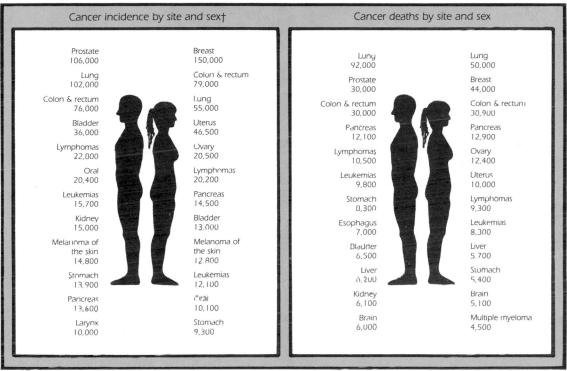

Cancer incidence by site and sex†		Cancer deaths by site and sex	
Prostate 106,000	Breast 150,000	Lung 92,000	Lung 50,000
Lung 102,000	Colon & rectum 79,000	Prostate 30,000	Breast 44,000
Colon & rectum 76,000	Lung 55,000	Colon & rectum 30,000	Colon & rectum 30,900
Bladder 36,000	Uterus 46,500	Pancreas 12,100	Pancreas 12,900
Lymphomas 22,000	Ovary 20,500	Lymphomas 10,500	Ovary 12,400
Oral 20,400	Lymphomas 20,200	Leukemias 9,800	Uterus 10,000
Leukemias 15,700	Pancreas 14,500	Stomach 8,300	Lymphomas 9,300
Kidney 15,000	Bladder 13,000	Esophagus 7,000	Leukemias 8,300
Melanoma of the skin 14,800	Melanoma of the skin 12,800	Bladder 6,500	Liver 5,700
Stomach 13,900	Leukemias 12,100	Liver 6,200	Stomach 5,400
Pancreas 13,600	Oral 10,100	Kidney 6,100	Brain 5,100
Larynx 10,000	Stomach 9,300	Brain 6,000	Multiple myeloma 4,500

† Excluding non-melanoma skin cancer and carcinoma in situ.

© 1990 by American Cancer Society. Used by permission.

teens, cancer of the cervix is far more frequent than among girls who marry in their twenties or who never marry.

Cancer detection

The earlier a cancer can be detected, the better are the prospects for its cure. Once the growth has spread to adjacent tissues or metastasized to distant organs, eradication or control of the malignancy is much more difficult. Those who know that

cancers in general (30 percent of all cancers). Another group who should be careful is persons with a family history of cancer. A third group is people who have already had a cancer.

The chart on page 690 points out the early signals of a developing malignancy in the various tissues and organs of the body.

There are also a number of symptoms of cancer of a more general na-

689

Cancer danger signals

The telltale symptoms listed in the right-hand column suggest the possibility of cancer in the organs named on the left. Any time these symptoms appear, you should immediately arrange for an examination by your doctor.

Bladder	Blood in the urine; increase in the frequency of urination.
Bone	Local pain, tenderness; unusual thickening of bone; walking with an unexplained limp.
Blood (leukemia)	Vague symptoms: fever, pallor, blood spreading into the tissues.
Breast	Lump or deformity in the breast or nipple.
Cervix	Abnormal bleeding, spotting with blood, or abnormal discharge.
Colon and rectum	Bleeding from the rectum, change in bowel habits.
Esophagus	Difficulty in swallowing.
Kidney (in adult)	Blood in urine (usually without pain); loss of appetite, fatigue, and loss of weight.
Kidney (in three-year-olds or younger)	Firm, painless mass in one side of abdomen.
Larynx	Sudden, unexplained, progressive hoarseness; later, difficult breathing.
Lip	Warty growth; crusting ulcer or fissure (resting in a disklike, firm area).
Lung	Cough (particularly different from the usual smoker's cough); transient sneezing. Later, spitting blood.

(continued on the next page)

Mouth and tongue	An area of roughening; mild burning when eating highly seasoned foods. Later, ulceration.
Skin	A pimple or small sore fails to heal and gradually enlarges; an old skin lesion now begins to grow; a persistent lesion crusts but bleeds when the crust is removed; an old wart or mole changes size or color.
Stomach	Persistent distress in upper abdomen, loss of appetite, loss of weight.
Uterus	Episodes of vaginal bleeding unrelated to menstruation.

NOTE: Most cancers are not painful, at least in their early stages. Thousands of cancer victims have lost their lives needlessly because they waited too long before seeing their doctor, thinking that their lesion could not be cancer because it was not painful.

Some cancers do not give a warning signal; they develop "silently," and the best prospects of cure have passed by the time the symptoms appear. Hence the advice: *See your physician for a periodic cancer checkup.*

ture. While not specific for cancer alone, they certainly should be considered and immediately reported to your physician. These include:

- Loss of appetite
- Loss of weight—for no apparent reason
- Tiredness—more than expected
- Headaches—out of the ordinary, and recurring
- Vomiting—sudden attacks without feeling sick
- Pain—steady, in the bones or deeply placed
- Fever—low grade, continual
- Weakness and pallor

The American Cancer Society points out seven warning signs:

- Change in bowel or bladder habits
- A sore that does not heal
- Unusual bleeding or discharge
- Thickening or lump in the breast, or elsewhere
- Indigestion or difficulty in swallowing
- Obvious change in a wart or mole
- Nagging cough or hoarseness

Diagnostic procedures

Should you suspect that you have cancer, immediately see your physician. He will give you a thorough medical checkup. Denial of facts is a serious mistake. If you have a family background of cancer, discuss this with your doctor. Have you been exposed to a known cancer-producing agent, such as tobacco

691

smoke? Do you smoke, have you ever smoked, or have you lived in a smoke-filled environment at home or at work?

Your physician will carefully examine the suspected site of the lesion. A number of diagnostic procedures are available today, including X-rays, ultrasound, radioisotope scanning, CT scans, and laboratory analysis of specimens of blood, urine, and other body discharges. Depending on the possible site of the cancer, a **mammogram** of the breasts or a **Pap smear** of vaginal discharge is appropriate in women. Medical Resonance Imaging (MRI) is particularly helpful in the diagnosis of brain tumors. Instruments are also available to visually examine the colon, the bladder, the bronchial tree, and the esophagus and stomach. The conclusive test, of course, is a biopsy of the lesion that has been examined by a pathologist. Your physician may wish to consult with a specialist himself, or he may refer you to one.

If you have cancer

Many people's first reaction to a cancer diagnosis is consternation or even panic. Fortunately, modern methods of treatment have greatly changed the picture, and many forms of cancer respond to appropriate therapy. If you are diagnosed with cancer, the following steps will help you relate to the problem intelligently in spite of how you feel.

Face the facts

Face the reality of the situation and get council from your physician and friends. If you have any doubt as to the diagnosis, request a second opinion. You may wish a diagnostic study at a reputable medical center. But **do not waste time.**

Plan realistically

Become well informed about the particular kind of cancer you have. Contact the American Cancer Society, 777 Third Avenue, New York, NY 10017, or the society's office nearest your home. They will provide you with literature that discusses cancer in general and your particular type of cancer in detail. Make two plans for the immediate future: one in case the treatment is successful, and the other in case it is not. Arrange your personal affairs and your commitments accordingly.

Beware of nostrums

Because of the dread that attends the discovery that a person has cancer, the disease lends itself to exploitation by unscrupulous persons who claim to have access to a "cure" for malignancy. "Cancer cures" have come and gone for as long as the disease has been recognized. Cancer still persists, but the promoters and their cures have run their courses and disappeared.

Quackery in the field of cancer therapy is a multibillion dollar busi-

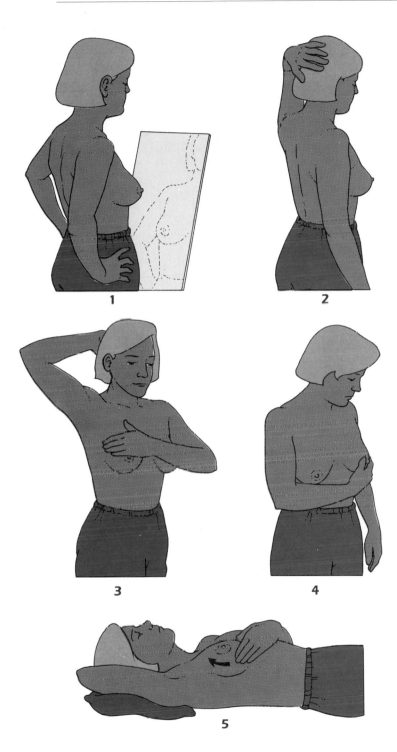

1

2

3

4

5

Self-examination of the breast.

You should examine your breasts once a month after your period. Check each breast in the following manner:

1. Stand in front of a mirror and drop your arms. Become familiar with the appearance of your breasts, the texture of the surface, and their size and shape. You should especially watch for changes. A rough texture may indicate a lump underneath.

2. Raise each arm above your head, and, turning from side to side, again watch for changes.

3. With your arm still raised above your head, press the flat of your hand against the surface of your breast. Check for changes in what you feel, especially lumps. Work your way around the entire breast.

4. Squeeze the nipple to see if there is a discharge.

5. Because the pressure of the tendons holding up your breasts when you stand may "hide" a lump, you should lie on your back with a pillow under your shoulders and check each breast again, following the instructions in number 3.

693

How to select your physician

Questionable therapy	Standard therapy
1. Practitioner is warm, friendly, and exudes confidence, but is not qualified by well-established specialty boards.	1. Practioner is qualified by well-established specialty boards.
2. Claims are carefully phrased and supported by testimonials, not by scientific research.	2. Claims are guarded and the treatment offered is supported by wide experience and research.
3. Diagnosis is made by unconventional methods. The results are not shared with other physicians.	3. Diagnosis is made by established procedures including biopsy. The results are gladly shared with other physicians.
4. The treatment is unique, and the practitioner claims regular physicians do not wish to use it because the cures would lose them money.	4. The therapy is not confined to a single individual or institution. The therapy is available at many medical centers.
5. The cost of therapy is high.	5. Costs are well established.
6. The surroundings are often exotic, as are the regime and diet.	6. The surroundings are not exotic, nor are the diet and procedures.
7. The practitioner claims that the government bans the therapy because of "big business."	7. The government and professional agencies cooperate to make the treatments available.
8. The practitioner and his support group exhibit a martyr or persecution complex.	8. There is an openness about all activities.

ness. Its promoters nearly always appear to be solicitous, warm, and caring. This, together with carefully-worded claims and voluminous support by testimonials (not research), often leads sufferers and their loved ones into spending precious time and large sums of money on questionable and unproven treatments. However, over and over again, this "can't lose" or "last resort" mentality has proven fatal to cancer victims.

Quacks frequently accuse the medical profession of refusing to use their particular therapy because of selfish reasons, and they indict the government for banning it out of support for "big business." They pay little attention to the fact that the American Cancer Society, the National Cancer Institute, and similar organizations in the United States and other countries are constantly evaluating every possible agent claimed to be effective in the treatment of cancer.

It would be bad enough if the loss of the sufferer's finances and those of his family were the only consideration. Unfortunately, all too often these irregular cures cause the cancer victim to neglect tried methods of treatment. Meanwhile, the cancer steadily progresses, reaching a stage where any treatment becomes hopeless. Thus many lives have been needlessly sacrificed.

While it is sometimes difficult for a professional, let alone a lay person, to evaluate the claims for a particular cancer cure, there are some serious questions you can ask regarding any purported remedy for cancer.

- Does the effectiveness of the remedy rest on testimonials of those supposedly cured, and on statements released to the news media by its promoters? If so, it should raise a serious doubt in your mind.

- Check to see whether the academic degrees the promoter claims to have are real. Is he a graduate of a bona fide academic institution? If he gives you the name of such an institution, call the university's public relations officer and ask whether he is really an alumnus. (The title "Doctor" applies to a number of degrees. Even the use of "M.D." is no assurance of valid qualifications, since this degree can be "bought" in certain countries.) Also call your local medical society and the American Cancer Society and ask about that person's professional standing among his peers. Another source of valuable information is the local office of the federal government's Food and Drug Administration. Their people can tell you the status of the remedy that is being recommended to you.

- What experience has this health practitioner had in diagnosing and treating malignancies? If he says you have a cancer, what tests did he employ, and how willing is he to share his findings with your physician? If he is, ask him to send your physician or pathologist a report for evaluation.

- Has this person published his findings in a reputable scientific journal, or is his literature in the form of *self-published* books, pamphlets, and papers?

- Is the treatment you are being offered found only in a distant geographical location (some other country) where surveillance by reputable professionals and government agencies does not exist?
- Does the promoter of this cure have a "secret formula" that he has promised some now deceased researcher to not disclose?
- Does he have a "martyr complex"? That is, did he have to leave the United States, or some other country with high medical standards, because his "remedy" would put regular medical practitioners out of business?
- Does he claim that he is being persecuted, and forced to "practice" where he is, because of his desire to help humanity?

Some years ago, a substance called *laetrile,* derived from apricot seeds, was widely promoted for its ability to cure cancer. It was heralded as a "natural remedy" and given the designation of a "missing vitamin" (vitamin B_{17}). Laetrile is amygdalin, a chemical that contains 6 percent cyanide by weight. A single 500 mg dose contains enough cyanide to kill a person if the cyanide were released from its chemical combination. Fortunately, most of a dose of laetrile is excreted without being broken into its constituent chemicals.

A study of nearly 200 laetrile treated cancer patients by independent researchers failed to show a single case in which there was a clear-cut anticancer benefit. Since laetrile costs very little to produce, the promoters did very well financially. During a twenty-seven month period, the documented bank deposits of one promoter totaled $2.5 million!

Cooperate in your treatment plan

Different types of cancer have differing treatment programs. Place yourself in the hands of a specialist in the treatment of your particular cancer. Your family physician can recommend the right person for you, as can the local medical society or the American Cancer Society.

Treatment of cancer

Your treatment may involve surgery, radiation, or chemotherapy, or a combination of these procedures. Depending on the malignancy, a hormonal therapy may be used.

When **surgery** is employed, the cancerous lesion and the surrounding tissues are removed. This is especially true if the cancer is discovered early, and while it is still localized. On occasion, surgery is preceded by radiation or chemotherapy—treatments used to reduce the size of the malignancy.

Irradiation therapy consists of exposing the tumor to X-rays or other forms of radiation. Modern techniques carefully direct the rays, concentrating them almost exclusively on the cancer, so that far less normal tissue adjacent to the cancer is destroyed. As a result, radiation sickness is now much less severe than in the past.

Chemotherapy employs chemical agents that destroy rapidly multiplying cells. These agents are used when the cancer is not localized, such as in leukemia. It is also used in cases when the cancer has been surgically removed but the possibility exists that some spread may have occurred, and when the cancer has already spread to so many areas of the body that the use of irradiation and surgery are not feasible. And, as already mentioned, chemotherapy may be used as a pretreatment to surgery.

In **hormonal therapy,** hormones or their synthetic counterparts are used to suppress the growth of cancers whose cells arose from endocrine organs, and are thus susceptible to the influence of these substances.

Medical specialists have long looked forward to the development of **immunotherapy**—treatment in which a person is protected from developing cancer by activating his own immune defenses. Newer immunotherapy techniques are proving to be effective in the treatment of certain animal tumors, and there is considerable optimism that similar approaches will soon be available in the fight against human cancer.

Below are a few examples of treatments directed against particular types of cancer that illustrate how the various therapeutic measures are used.

Lung cancer. No uniformly effective treatment for lung cancer exists, though early surgical removal of the affected portion of the lung, sometimes supplemented by irradiation therapy and/or chemotherapy, saves up to about 10 percent of cases.

Breast cancer. For cancer of the breast, the current trend is to use surgery conservatively, followed by irradiation to kill cancer cells that may remain in the region of the breast, and chemotherapy to suppress or prevent the growth of cancer cells that may have migrated to other parts of the body.

Leukemia. With leukemias (cancer of the blood-forming tissues) chemotherapy, sometimes supplemented by irradiation therapy, gives the best results.

Prostate cancer. Hormone therapy is especially useful in treating this cancer.

Preventing cancer—what you can do

The best "treatment" for cancer is to avoid it in the first place. Many experts believe that up to 90 percent of all cancer is due at least in part to environmental or lifestyle exposures, and that most, if not all, of these could be avoided.

One of your best precautions is a complete medical checkup by your physician on a regular basis, especially as you get older. Women should request a Pap smear at least as often as they have a regular checkup, and occasionally a mammogram.

We have already mentioned tobacco, alcohol, and caffeine (the chemical found in coffee, tea, many soft drinks, and mate [mah-teh]—a popular South American drink) as potential cancer producers. Cigarette smoke is the single greatest culprit in many of today's societies. Unfortunately, cigarette smoke is intimately associated with the use of alcohol and coffee drinking, and these in turn may all be linked directly or indirectly to dietary factors.

Some researchers maintain that approximately two-thirds of all cancer deaths can be ascribed to tobacco and diet. They believe that in the United States diet plays the major role in female cancer, while tobacco is the primary cause of cancer in men. Dietary fats, especially those derived from animal sources (fatty steaks, lard, butter) may promote cancerous growths in the tissues of the breast and the lining of the colon. It also appears that animal protein may increase the risk of cancers of the prostate, colon, and kidneys.

Cancer of the colon is rare in people with a diet that is high in fiber and low in animal protein, fat, and refined sugar. In such diets, the passage of waste through the intestinal tract (called transit time) is significantly shorter than it is for people who eat the typical Western diet. A high-fiber diet also changes the mix of intestinal organisms, and it appears that the extra bulk provided by the fiber may dilute carcinogens and co-carcinogens, making them less effective. In these and other ways, high dietary fiber reduces the risk of colon and rectal cancer (see also page 92).

For these reasons it would seem wise, as you plan your diet, to avoid refined foods from which much of the fiber has been removed. Choose foods that are low in fat (especially fat of animal origin) and that have low to moderate amounts of protein. Plant proteins are best. Obese women have a higher incidence of breast cancer than women of normal weight, so you should plan on just enough calories to avoid becoming overweight (see page 231).

Use common-sense measures to avoid or minimize exposure to chemicals in your home, garage, garden, and workplace. For example, avoid inhaling aerosol sprays such as hair spray, insect repellent, lubricant, and home cleaner. Also, avoid all unnecessary contact with laundry detergents, polishes, gasoline, oils, and chemicals at large. Be sure to wear a mask any time you must use pesticides and other sprays, and thoroughly wash your skin when you are through to remove contaminants.

Recent research indicates that a healthy body has several methods of blocking certain cancer-causing events. Your body has a mechanism that prevents the transformation of a normal cell into a cancer cell, and even when such a transformation has occurred, the newly formed cancer cell and its offspring may be destroyed. Thus a healthy lifestyle (see page 117) is a preventive not only for cancer, but also for many of the other killer diseases so common in our society.

Here is a summary of things that you can do to lower your risk of getting cancer:

- **Avoid exposure to known cancer-producing agents.** These include tobacco smoke, beverage alcohol, caffeine-containing drinks, aerosols, paints and solvents, poison sprays, excessive sunshine, and unnecessary X-ray radiation.
- **Dietary cautions.** Eat plenty of fruits and vegetables, especially broccoli, cabbage, brussels sprouts, and other green leafy vegetables. Eat whole grain cereals and some legumes (beans) to ensure a generous intake of fiber.

  Do not overeat, and if you are overweight, regain your normal weight. Reduce your intake of fat to 15 to 20 percent of your total calories. If you are an average American, this means cutting your fat intake to a little less than half what it now is. Where possible, replace red meat with fish, or, even better, with milk and vegetable proteins. Most cheeses are high in fat.
- **Maintain physical well-being.** These are discussed under a healthful lifestyle.
- **Maintain mental well-being.** Studies have shown that happy people—especially those who are very happy—live much longer than those who are unhappy. "Laughter wards" have actually been established in many hospitals today, because of the healing benefit of cheerfulness. The Good Book says, "A merry heart doeth good like a medicine" (Proverbs 17:22). Trust God. Try to help someone who has greater needs than you do, and be grateful for the blessings you do have.

Cancers at large

The cancers that occur in the various tissues and organs of the body are described in detail under the diseases of each organ or system. They are also listed in the general index.

CHAPTER 24

General infections

The human body is veritably bathed in an ocean of germs: bacteria, viruses, and fungi. While most are friendly or harmless, some are hostile and dangerous. A newborn baby is sterile, but immediately upon birth it is invaded by countless microorganisms. Fungal spores in the air and the touch of helping hands and loving lips soon blanket the infant in germs. On the skin, in the hair follicles, up the nose, down the throat, in the intestinal tract, and on and in the external sex organs, microscopic and submicroscopic invaders establish residence.

Infection refers to the entrance into the body's tissues of disease-producing organisms. To gain this entrance they must cross one of two barriers: the skin or the mucous membranes. The skin is covered by an acid coat that hampers the growth of microbes, both bacteria and fungi, while the normal inhabitants of the skin are also hostile to any newcomers. The mucous membranes are no less defensive, as their fluid secretions are toxic to numerous germs. Mucus and other watery secretions pour from countless glands embedded in the membranes of the respiratory, digestive, and genito-urinary tracts.

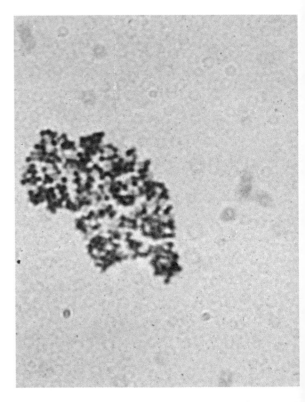

Staphylococcal germs (highly magnified).

The respiratory tract filters the air you breathe. The tortuous path that air must follow after it is breathed traps dust and associated germs. The mucus that lines the bronchial passages traps additional germs, and by means of the mucus elevator (see page 902) expels it into the mouth, where it is either spat out or swallowed. Coughing clears the respiratory tree of large accumulations of mucus and debris.

The digestive tract provides an inhospitable environment to germs. The highly acid secretions of the stomach act as a chlorinating plant that kills many organisms. The contents of the stomach, including germs, move into the highly alkaline small intestine, where concentrated bile and digestive enzymes destroy additional germs. Mucus also flows from the intestinal walls, and the wavelike contractions of the walls sweep the contents of the intestine downward into the colon, where all newcomers in the germ population must defend themselves against es-tablished residents or be carried out in the stool. The urinary and genital tracts of both men and women are also designed to resist the inroads of germs. Many of their secretions contain anti-infective constituents.

Should the skin break or a mucous membrane be breached, the microbes face another formidable line of defense in the tissues and the circulating blood that is designed to combat any invasion by disease-producing organisms. Phagocytic cells (cells that surround germs and foreign particles) can engulf invading germs like giant vacuum sweepers, and even destroy them. Any microbe that escapes the phagocytic cells must still face chemical warfare as the body's immune mechanisms (see page 827) come into play. Each unfriendly germ stimulates the production of specific antibodies and other lethal chemicals that have been custom-made to combat it. The body makes every possible effort to expel or destroy every foreign invader.

As the invaders and the defense

Injuries may introduce disease-producing organisms into the body.

701

forces lock in mortal combat, certain factors tend to swing the outcome in either a favorable or unfavorable direction. Sometimes the enemy's superior numbers overwhelm the body's defenses. At other times the defense forces are more deadly in their attack.

The individual's relative susceptibility is another variable. Immunity is one of the body's strongest defenses against invading microbes. For example, anyone who has recovered from rubella has antibodies within his system that protect him for the remainder of his life from any future illness caused by this particular virus, but the person whose tissues do not contain these antibodies may become an easy victim once the virus has breached his defenses.

On the other hand, fatigue, malnourishment, or other illnesses reduce the efficiency of the body's defense system, making the person more susceptible to infections. Even mental attitudes can affect the defense system. Immunity is enhanced in people who are happy and contented while anger and resentment diminish resistance. The old saying has been proved true today: "A merry heart doeth good like a medicine, but a broken spirit drieth the bones" (Proverbs 17:22).

Local infections

Should infective organisms break through the defenses at some particular site, every effort is made to limit, or localize, the spread of the infection. Soldier cells called phagocytes (white blood cells) pour into the infected area, "closing ranks" to

A pimple or small boil is a localized infection in the skin.

literally wall off the zone of conflict. When this occurs in tissue that is near the surface of the body, the resulting local infection is called a **boil,** or on a smaller scale, a **pimple.** Virulent germs may destroy some of the tissue. This tissue debris, together with dead germs, active germs, and phagocytes, fills the center of the mass, forming what we call **pus.**

A similar scenario occurs when a local infection develops deeper inside the body, but the localized infection is called an **abscess.** In both boils and abscesses, the contents of the infection must be evacuated, or they may be reabsorbed. Evacuation occurs when a boil bursts or an abscess is surgically lanced and drained. Squeezing a boil or pimple may actually spread the infection by forcing germs into surrounding tissue.

General infections

When invading microorganisms overwhelm the body's defense

702

forces, or when some of them slip past the body's blockade, they are usually entrapped by the lymphatic system (see page 828). The lymph (tissue fluid), together with the invading germs, is carried by tiny vessels to the lymph nodes, where the invaders must run the gauntlet of additional defense cells. The lymph nodes may enlarge as additional forces are brought in to fight the enemy.

Despite these efforts, germs frequently do enter the bloodstream (**bacteremia, septicemia**—the presence of hostile microorganisms in the blood). These meet additional "lines of defense" in the cells of the liver, spleen (reticulo-endothelial), and lungs (phagocytic) that attack and destroy the invaders. Germs may enter the blood during the treatment of local infections, such as the extraction of an infected tooth or the draining of an abscess. On very rare occasions invaders from these sources can cause serious infections such as endocarditis, osteomyelitis, and brain abscess. To avoid this danger, the physician may prescribe antibiotics.

Infectious and contagious diseases

An **infectious disease** is a disease caused by a germ or virus that enters the body. Malaria, caused by a parasite, is an example of an infectious disease. By contrast, atherosclerosis is not caused by a microorganism and is not an infectious disease. A **contagious disease** is an infectious disease that can be easily transmitted from a sick person to a well person,

usually by close contact. Syphilis is an example of such a disease. Sometimes contagious diseases are spoken of as **communicable diseases.**

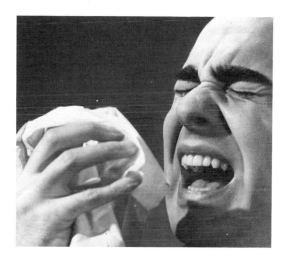

Many infectious diseases are spread by droplets carrying germs and viruses that are discharged into the air by sneezing and coughing.

Responses to infections

Toxins from an infection, circulated through the body, may prompt chills (ague) and fever. This occurs, for instance, when the malarial parasite is released from the red blood cells during one phase of the disease. Fever is a uniform accompaniment of many serious infectious diseases. In some cases the rise in body temperature aids the body's defenses in combating the infection.

Infection and other diseases may alter the "thermostat" setting in the brain, impairing its effectiveness, and causing the body temperature to rise. When this happens we say that the patient has a fever. Delirium may result anytime the temperature rises above 105°F. In infants and young children high temperatures may precipitate convulsions, making it necessary to take steps to lower the temperature. This can include tepid baths, with or without medication.

Another response to infection is the rise in the number and type of certain white blood cells in the blood, and also in the immediate vicinity of the source of the infection, as in septic sore throat.

Infections that the body can overcome if given enough time are called **self-limited.** Should the body's defenses prove inadequate, the illness may be prolonged, or the outcome may be fatal. When the defense is adequate, the organisms are overcome, the disease is terminated, and health is restored.

Therapy for infections

Two principles underline the treatment of infections: (1) reinforcement and augmentation of the body's own defense mechanisms and (2) weakening or destroying the invaders by physical or chemical means.

The body must ultimately heal itself. Providing adequate rest and sleep, simple diet, abundant fluids (often provided intravenously), a quiet environment, and certain physical therapy procedures (see page 589) aid the body's defenses. Sometimes antibodies (immune globulins) and antitoxins (in tetanus) greatly accelerate recovery.

Anti-infective agents attack the invaders by making them more vulnerable to the body's defenses by killing them. The antibiotic penicillin weakens the cell wall surrounding the pneumococci bacteria (which causes one form of pneumonia), causing it to die. Quinine is directly toxic to the malarial parasite.

Prevention

Maintaining health by means of a healthful lifestyle (see page 117) is the most effective and cheapest protection against infectious diseases. Life is such that we cannot live in a sealed environment that does not allow us to be exposed to germs and viruses. These would-be villains envelop us and are but waiting for an opportunity to strike. Health, good health, is best maintained by having a high regard for nature's laws. Such a lifestyle will maximize our resistance to infectious germs and minimize our risk of disease.

coils and the smooth muscle contracts, the ball of blood passes down the arterial tree. The pressure required by the heart and arteries to accomplish this is called the **blood pressure.**

When a doctor examines you, he is interested, among other things, in finding what your blood pressure is. This he does by placing an inflatable cuff around your arm (just above your elbow), connecting a gauge to the cuff, and listening through a stethoscope placed just below the crease in front of your elbow. He then inflates the cuff. As the cuff becomes tighter and tighter, it acts like a tourniquet, squeezing the arm so tightly that the blood can no longer flow through the artery to reach your forearm. The sound of the blood flow ceases.

The physician now slowly releases the pressure in the cuff until the first sounds of blood flow are noted. By watching the pressure gauge, he can read the pressure at this moment. When the pressure within the cuff no longer restricts the flow of blood through the artery, the sounds of your heartbeats can no longer be heard. The pressure at this point is again recorded.

These two readings, the high and the low, are called the **systolic** and **diastolic** pressures. The systolic pressure is the highest pressure that the heart produces as it pumps blood into the arteries at the time of a heartbeat. The lowest reading represents the pressure that remains in the arteries just before the next heartbeat takes place.

In a normal, healthy young adult whose heart is working properly and whose blood vessels are not diseased, the systolic pressure is usually about 120 and the diastolic pressure about 80. This is commonly written as 120/80. These figures indicate the height, in millimeters, of a column of mercury if the other end of the tube were connected to the artery.

By the time the blood reaches the capillaries it is flowing slowly. This slow movement of blood through the capillaries allows time for the oxygen and food nutrients to enter the tissues and for the carbon dioxide and waste materials to enter the blood. The blood in the large arteries may move at a speed of about 100 feet (30 meters) per minute, which is more than a thousand times as fast as it moves through the capillaries. A drop of blood takes about two seconds to pass through a capillary which is about .025 inch (6 millimeters) long, and will be back in the heart, from a distant part of the body, within half a minute!

The level of blood pressure throughout your body and the volume of blood flow in any local region of the body are precisely influenced by the autonomic (or automatic) nervous system. This is accomplished by stimulating the smooth muscle in the arterioles. Contraction of these muscles narrows the caliber of the arteries, resulting in an increase in blood pressure.

The blood pressure in your body varies from time to time, and even from place to place. When you stand, your blood pressure is higher in your

771

legs than in your arms. It rises slightly when you sit up from lying down, or stand up from sitting. When you exert yourself, such as lifting a heavy suitcase or exercising vigorously, your blood pressure rises to met the demand for blood in the muscles involved in these tasks. During digestion, the digestive organs need more blood. This increase is provided by a reduction of the flow of blood to other parts of the body so that a correspondingly greater volume of blood flows through the digestive organs. When you are engaged in active thinking, the flow of blood through the brain accelerates slightly.

Blood pressure and the heart rate rise during emergencies, as the muscles attaching to the bones (skeletal muscles) are alerted to possible action. When you are frightened, your blood pressure rises, putting a greater workload on your heart and artery walls. But emergencies should be but for short periods. People who are nervous, anxious, and fearful tend to maintain a higher than desirable blood pressure. This may lead to serious problems (see under "high blood pressure" or "hypertension" on page 785). Generally a consistent pressure of 140/80 is considered borderline hypertension.

Blood

The **blood**, carried within the blood vessels, is the main transport system of the body. On the outward journey, blood brings the cells oxygen, nutrients, and chemical substances essential for their proper functioning. On its return trip, blood removes cellular wastes.

Your blood, some 10 to 11 pints in volume, consists of blood cells, or corpuscles, floating in a yellowish liquid called plasma. Plasma also contains a variety of salts, fats, proteins, hormones, blood sugar, blood-clotting agents, and antibodies. The major wastes are carbon dioxide and urea.

Six types of cells normally seen in the blood.

There are two kinds of blood cells: red and white. The **red cells** or erythrocytes number some 25 to 30 trillion in an adult, and outnumber the white cells about 600 to one. Smaller than white cells, they live about 120 days. To replace those that wear out, the bone marrow must produce about 200 billion new red cells daily, or from 2 to 3 million every second, twenty-four hours a day—and more if you have lost blood or given a

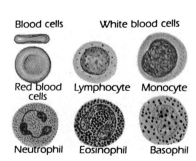

Blood cells   White blood cells

Red blood cells   Lymphocyte   Monocyte

Neutrophil   Eosinophil   Basophil

transfusion! Your body is an incredible structure and should never be taken for granted.

The major function of red cells is to carry oxygen from the lungs to the body cells, and carbon dioxide from the cells back to the lungs. The remarkable substance making this transfer—a red iron-containing pigment called hemoglobin—gives blood its red color.

The five different types of **white cells** constitute part of the body's police force, defending it against disease and any foreign invader. The bone marrow produces three different granulocytes that travel to all parts of the body hunting for trouble. They live a very short time because they often die fighting the enemy. In cases of infection or injury to the tissues, the white cells gather in large numbers to help prevent the spread of infection and to aid in the process of healing.

The bone marrow also produces a fourth type of white cell—a macrophage or monocyte. This large cell is a front-line defender and acts like a vacuum sweeper, engulfing debris entering the bloodstream. Encountering any foreign organisms, such as bacteria or viruses, it alerts the defense forces.

A fifth type of white blood cell is the lymphocyte, produced and stored in the lymph glands or lymph nodes, which is part of the lymphatic system. Lymphocytes also provide a defense against bacteria and foreign substances. Some of these are extremely long-lived, and once exposed to certain disease agents or foreign substances, they store this "biological information" for years or a lifetime.

The body's marvelous defense mechanisms against an aggressor are still but partially understood. Here are some of the more obvious defense steps. A virus enters a cell. Immediately a macrophage moves over and engulfs the stricken cell. By some mysterious method of communication it immediately summons a helper T cell to the scene. This cell identifies the enemy and takes command of the defense forces. In the spleen and other lymph nodes it orders the production of killer T cells to fight the enemy. These killer T cells attack the cells that have been invaded.

The helper T cells also mobilize other lymphocytes, called B cells, to increase in numbers and to produce potent chemical substances called antibodies. These Y-shaped protein molecules rush to the site of infection. Here the antibodies either neutralize the enemy or mark it for attack by other defense cells or chemicals.

As an infection is overcome, another type of T cell slows down or stops the production and activity of B cells and T cells, bringing the defense forces to an on-duty peacetime footing. Formed sometime during the battle with the enemy, a so-called "memory cell" develops, which may travel in the blood or lymph for years. It is capable of immediately identifying the enemy and quickly mobilizing the body's defenses.

Platelets, small fragments of larger cells called megakaryocytes, are formed in the bone marrow. When a blood vessel wall is injured or

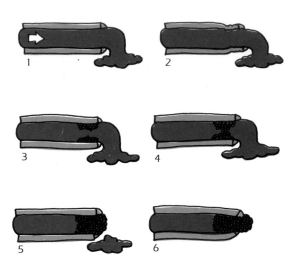

broken, permitting the loss of blood, platelets accumulate at the site of the damage. They stick to the injured surfaces and break apart, releasing a special chemical that stimulates the formation of tiny threads of fibrin, a protein present in the blood. The tangled mass of fibrin threads entraps blood cells in its meshes, and together with them forms a clot. This prevents further loss of blood from the cut or injured vessel. Circulating platelets live an average of ten days.

Steps in clot formation: (1) vessel when first cut, (2) cut end constricts and retracts, (3) platelets stick to injured surfaces, (4) fibrin appears, (5) clot forms in four to five minutes, (6) clot retracts within an hour.

Blood types or groups

Even though the blood from one person looks just like that from another person, it may differ significantly. Persons of the same race or even of the same family may have different "types" of blood. The genes you inherited from your parents determine your **blood type.**

On the surface of each person's red blood cells are specific protein molecules called **antigens,** and equally specific **antibodies** in the

Blood types and their frequencies				
Type	Antigen	Antibodies	Percent	Class
A	A	B	40	
B	B	A	10	
AB	A, B	none	5	Universal recipients
O	none	A, B	45	Universal donors

plasma. The chart on page 774 summarizes the four common blood types: A, B, AB, and O with their major characteristics.

Another system of blood classification has to do with whether an Rh antigen is present. About 85 percent of the people in the United States have this factor in their blood and are said to be "Rh positive." The remaining 15 percent are Rh negative.

A person who is Rh negative cannot tolerate Rh positive blood given as a transfusion. Such a mistake causes serious damage to the kidneys, with possible death. The reason is that the Rh negative person builds up antibodies that destroy the cells of the Rh positive blood. A further complication occurs when a woman with Rh negative blood becomes pregnant with a child who happens to have Rh positive blood.

Blood transfusions

In cases of severe hemorrhage, injury, certain types of surgery, and other situations in which it becomes necessary to restore or replace a person's blood, the transfusion of blood from another person (or from the same person given by himself in advance) may prove to be lifesaving.

If you need a transfusion, it is imperative that you be given blood that is compatible with your blood type. The donor's blood must be matched with yours in the laboratory to be sure that it is correct. If you receive the wrong type, your antibodies will attack the antigens in the donor's (incoming) blood, causing the donor's red blood cells to stick together (agglutinate), and the result could be kidney failure, shock, or even death. For example, if you are a type A, you cannot receive type B blood because your antibodies will attack the antigens in the incoming red blood cells. However, if you are type AB, you do not have antibodies to be triggered by the antigens of the blood you receive, and you will have no reaction. You are called a universal recipient. That means you can receive blood from any donor. People with type O blood are universal donors. That is, they can donate their blood to anyone, because they have no antigens to trigger the antibodies in the people to whom they donate. However, type O can only receive blood from another person with type O blood.

If you do not know your blood type, your physician can order a blood test that will tell you. The percent column tells approximately what percent of the population has that particular blood type (the type in the left-hand column).

Human blood cannot be manufactured outside the human body. Therefore healthy people interested in helping to save lives donate blood to be stored in blood banks for emergencies. The average adult can give one pint (450 ml) of blood at a time without endangering his health, provided he does not do it too often. It takes the donor's body about six weeks to regenerate this amount of blood.

CHAPTER 2

Disorders of the heart and blood vessels

Cardiovascular disease accounts for more than one third of all deaths in the developed nations of the world. The two most common forms of this disease are coronary heart disease and high blood pressure (hypertension). Another, stroke, is close behind. In the United States, for example, one out of every eight Americans has one or more of these diseases, with coronary heart disease being the number one killer. In Japan stroke is the leading cause of death.

In the Western world more people suffer and die from heart disease than from any other ailment. The most common vascular ailments—coronary heart disease, hypertension or high blood pressure, and stroke—account for close to a million deaths annually.

The underlying cause of these and other fairly common heart and blood vessel diseases is largely a disease process of the arteries called atherosclerosis. Since athero-sclerosis is a form of arterio-sclerosis, it will be discussed first. Until some forty years ago, people generally believed that heart disease was a natural result of aging, of some infectious disease such as rheumatic fever, or of heredity.

However, from the careful observation of the lifestyle of large groups of people, researchers have identified certain circumstances and conditions, called "risk factors," that cause people to be more susceptible to atherosclerosis and, as a result, to heart attacks. These risk factors, some major and others minor, some controllable and others not, are listed below and briefly discussed.

While the presence or absence of risk factors does not absolutely predict one's susceptibility to a heart attack, experience has shown that the more risk factors a person has, the more likely the occurrence of a coronary. Obviously, then, a person is wise to analyze his lifestyle and make

Risk factors	
Controllable	**Uncontrollable**
Major	
High blood cholesterol	Age
High blood pressure	Sex
Cigarette smoking	Heredity
Minor	
Emotional stress	
Lack of exercise	
Obesity	
Type A personality	
Diabetes	

a determined effort to eliminate as many of the risk factors as possible. Since lifestyles and risk factors will be discussed in more detail elsewhere, only a brief summary will be given here.

Controllable risk factors

Cholesterol, which is manufactured by the body, is a normal constituent of the cells and blood, and is actually essential to life itself. The problem arises when the amount in the body, as noted by the level in the blood, becomes excessive. Interestingly, foods of plant origin—fruits, vegetables, grains, and nuts—contain no cholesterol. But it is found in generous amounts in foods of animal origin—meat, fish, fowl, milk, and especially eggs, seafoods, and organ meats. Thus excessive levels of

cholesterol in the blood result from the overmanufacture of cholesterol by the body or by unwise dietary practices, among other things.

Cholesterol, a fatlike substance, is attached to a protein, called lipoprotein, that is carried in the blood. The various lipoproteins are classified according to their densities. Very low density lipoproteins (VLDL), low density (LDL), and high density (HDL). HDL or "good" cholesterol is believed to carry fats out of the cells of the body and to protect the artery walls from atherosclerosis. LDL or "bad" cholesterol is thought to be the prime culprit in developing atherosclerosis. The higher the ratio of HDL to LDL, the better off the person is. For practical purposes, however, the total amount of cholesterol in the blood forms a good index of the person's susceptibility to atherosclerosis.

The level of cholesterol in the blood varies from time to time and from day to day in the same person, so for a precise determination a cholesterol test should be done more than once. However, a single test provides a valuable target range. Generally a level of 170 milligrams per 100 milliliters of blood (170 mg per 100 ml) or below is considered a good or "safe" level. But actually no absolutely safe or normal value exists, for with any value above 125 milligrams per 100 milliliters the risk increases. The average American has a blood cholesterol level of about 225 milligrams per 100 milliliters. With a value of 250 milligrams compared to 175 milligrams, the risk rises fourfold. With levels greater than 300,

777

the risk of a coronary increases eight or more times.

High blood pressure (hypertension) occurs when the pressure within the arteries is consistently maintained above 140/85 while a person is at rest. Such pressures, over a period of years, will damage the walls of the arteries and contribute to their hardening (arteriosclerosis). Hardening of the coronary arteries of the heart results in diminished flow and places the person at a higher risk of a coronary.

Cigarette smoking, another major risk factor, greatly increases the risk of a heart attack. A number of constituents of tobacco smoke enter the blood, affecting the heart and blood vessels. Nicotine directly affects the heart, causing it to beat faster. At the same time it constricts or narrows the smaller arteries, thus raising the blood pressure, reducing available blood to the heart, and increasing the heart's workload. Carbon monoxide, a gas present in cigarette smoke, enters the blood, combining more strongly with hemoglobin than does oxygen. This displaces some of the oxygen which the blood normally carries, so the heart gets less oxygen for its needs while at the same time nicotine is making it work harder.

Beyond this, nicotine causes the body to react as it would to stress. Adrenaline (epinephrine) is secreted into the blood, increasing the heart rate, raising both the blood pressure and the level of cholesterol. The junction points of the cells lining the arteries buckle, allowing cholesterol and other lipoproteins to enter the walls, initiating, as some think, the process of atherosclerosis. While filter-tip cigarettes may slightly reduce the amount of nicotine entering the body, they may actually increase the concentration of carbon monoxide!

Emotional stress is part of everyday living, but when the level is high and its occurrence frequent, serious problems may arise. Stress is the body's response to some event or situation perceived to be undesirable or harmful. The responses parallel those of fear and anger—the "fight or flight" response—in which the body gears for action to stand up and meet the problem or to try to escape it. The heart speeds up; blood pressure rises; muscles tense; in the blood the levels of blood sugar, blood fats, and cholesterol rise; and adrenalin pours into the blood, which now clots more readily. The person feels fearful or anxious, tense, and nervous. Persons with type A personalities and others who respond adversely to everyday stresses are at a higher risk for a heart attack.

As with nicotine, so with stress. Cholesterol enters the artery walls where the junction points of cells lining the arteries buckle.

Lack of exercise is another major risk factor. Exercise strengthens the heart and blood vessels as the active muscles make demands for more oxygen and fuel. Inactivity, on the other hand, weakens the cardiovascular system and at the same time increases the occurrence of other risk factors such as obesity, hypertension, elevated cholesterol, and nervous tension.

Obesity, like sedentary living, is also considered a major risk factor. The workload of the heart increases, since blood has to be pumped through hundreds of miles of extra blood vessels to keep alive the pounds of extra body mass. Obesity is closely associated with hypertension, diabetes, elevated blood fats, and cholesterol.

Diabetes or "sugar diabetes" results from the body's inability to utilize insulin efficiently or from the production of insufficient amounts. Blood sugar rises to undesirable levels, and some spills over into the urine. High blood levels of fats (triglycerides) and cholesterol, along with atherosclerosis and arteriosclerosis, are common. Precise control by appropriate medication (insulin or insulin substitutes) and by diet and exercise is essential to avoid greatly increasing the risk of heart attack.

Uncontrollable risk factors

Age does not of itself cause heart disease. Instead, the slow destruction of the arterial wall with gradual narrowing that occurs over a period of twenty to thirty years may eventually result in a heart attack. So it is not surprising to find that heart disease is more common in older people. Many older people have strong, healthy hearts because their lifestyle avoided or minimized the controllable risk factors. Occasionally one hears of an individual who lives to a ripe old age and has done everything he shouldn't! However, nature's endowment of a robust cardiovascular system should get the credit, not his way of life.

Sex. Men are generally more prone to heart attacks than are women, especially males thirty-five to fifty years of age. Several factors appear to favor women. Female hormones or estrogens seem to be protective, for within a few years after menopause the susceptibility of women equals that of men. Women tend to carry a higher IIDL level than men. And, until recently, women did not smoke to the same extent as did men. Unfortunately, this situation is changing.

Heredity. Some evidence exists that heart disease runs in families. A family record in which blood relatives have had coronary heart disease, especially between forty to fifty years of age, increases your risk of a heart attack. In some families very high cholesterol levels and/or high blood pressure appear to be inherited. These conditions add to the risk. Although you cannot choose your parents and close relatives, recognizing your inherited weaknesses and modifying your lifestyle may help you considerably.

Atherosclerosis

As already mentioned, arteries are musculo-elastic tubes that carry oxygen-laden blood to the tissues of the body. Their smooth inner lining minimizes friction. Sometimes fatty streaks appear on this inner lining, especially where the artery divides or is damaged. These streaks may enlarge, and muscle cells beneath them may multiply, causing the wall to bulge inward. This, in turn, sets up turbulence, which further dam-

779

ages the lining. The growing mass, which contains muscle cells, cholesterol, and calcium salts, along with fibrous tissue and collagen, is called an **atheroma** or **plaque.** The passageway is narrowed, blood flow is restricted, and if the process continues, the artery may become blocked. This hardening process, called **atherosclerosis,** contributes to a general form of hardening of the arteries called **arteriosclerosis,** and is the prime cause of coronary heart disease.

Although the causes of atherosclerosis are not fully understood, the disease is associated with elevated levels of blood cholesterol and blood fats. Certain lifestyle habits seem to be contributory: a diet rich in animal fats and cholesterol (fatty meats, butter, eggs, certain seafoods,

and organ meats), along with kidney failure and the other risk factors discussed above.

Symptoms. Since atherosclerosis occurs within an artery wall, the primary symptoms are disorders of the organ to which the artery provides blood. These symptoms appear as the blood supply to the affected organ is reduced, either gradually or abruptly.

If the arteries of your heart are affected, you may suffer from angina or a heart attack; if those of the brain, a stroke; if those of your legs, muscle cramps on walking, or if severe occlusion has developed, gangrene of your toes or foot. If your renal arteries are blocked, kidney failure will result.

An exception to this is the development of an aneurysm (see page 799) in the artery itself. Here

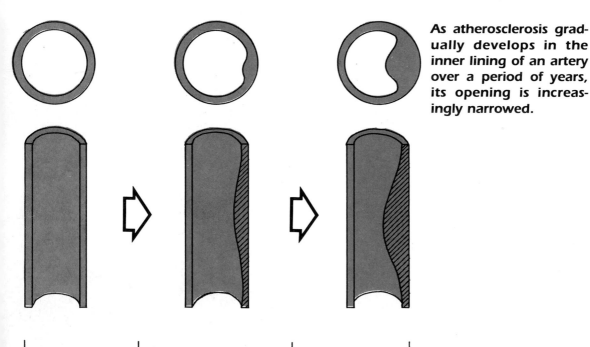

As atherosclerosis gradually develops in the inner lining of an artery over a period of years, its opening is increasingly narrowed.

Vessel narrowed over years

atherosclerosis has so weakened the artery wall that blood begins to seep between its layers, or the wall bursts.

What you can do. Since atherosclerosis develops over a period of years without any symptoms, when symptoms do appear, the process is well advanced. You should carefully evaluate your lifestyle and take the necessary steps to alter those factors that may lead to atherosclerosis (see under "risk factors," pages 777-779).

What your physician can do. Your physician can determine your blood pressure, the level of your cholesterol and blood fats (triglycerides), or whether your blood sugar is too high (diabetes). He can aid you with your diet and other lifestyle changes. He may recommend certain medications for conditions that do not respond to lifestyle changes.

Coronary heart disease (Ischemic heart disease, angina, heart attack)

An average healthy man living in the United States has about one chance in five of developing coronary heart disease before he reaches sixty-five. Notice that we mentioned the average *man*. Coronary heart disease is more common among men than among women.

Coronary heart disease accounts for practically all the instances of "heart attack" that strike suddenly.

Obstruction by a blood clot (thrombus) in a major branch of a coronary artery deprives a certain area of the heart wall of its blood supply, bringing on a heart attack (myocardial infarction).

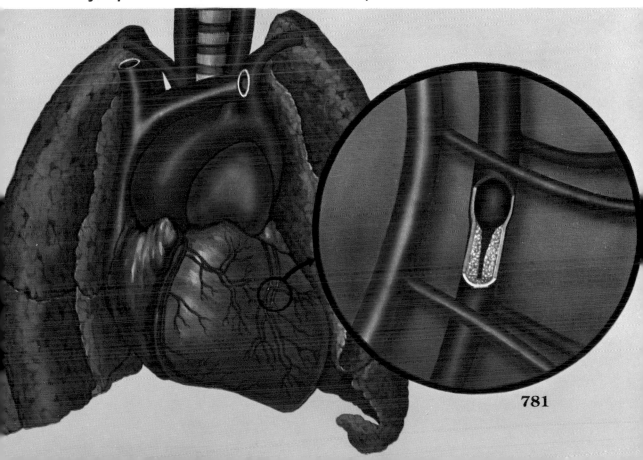

781

Of those suffering such an attack, 25 percent die within three hours. Another 10 percent die within the next four weeks. The survivors live with the knowledge that they remain vulnerable to another heart attack unless they drastically change their way of life.

Atherosclerosis is the basic cause of coronary heart disease. The coronary arteries are just as susceptible as any other arteries to the development of atherosclerosis. The right and left coronary arteries, as their name implies, encircle the heart like a crown, and supply the heart muscle with blood. As these arteries or their branches become blocked, the heart muscle they supply becomes deprived of oxygen. A state of myocardial ischemia occurs, with shortness of breath or chest pain (angina), especially on exertion or when a person is emotionally stressed. It is possible, however, to have ischemia of the heart muscle without pain.

Angina is a pain deep to the breastbone (angina pectoris) caused by a reduced flow of blood to some area of the heart muscle. It usually results from atherosclerosis in the wall of a coronary artery, though sometimes it is due to a spasm of the vessel. The pain, discomfort, or feeling of pressure or squeezing may be severe, and the intensity of the distress may vary. The pain may radiate to the shoulder and down the arm (usually on the left side), but may involve both arms, the neck, and even the lower face. These symptoms mimic those of a heart attack, but usually last only a few minutes and

are relieved by rest or a drug such as nitroglycerine.

What you can do. If it is your first attack, assume that the situation is the more serious of the two possibilities, a heart attack rather than angina, and see your physician immediately. If he is not available, call the fire department or an ambulance. Remain calm, cease all physical activity, and remain quietly at rest, lying on your back.

If you have had previous episodes you doubtless have nitroglycerine tablets; place one or two under your tongue. This should relieve your anginal pain. If the pain and discomfort persist for more than five

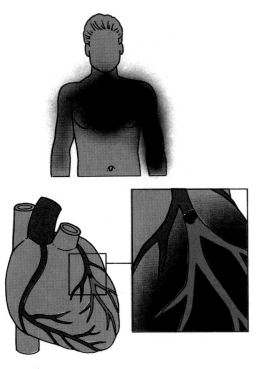

Restricted blood flow through a coronary artery may cause severe pain over the heart radiating to the shoulder, arm or arms, neck, and even the face.

782

minutes or become increasingly severe, you probably are having a heart attack, and the condition is very serious. Call for help. For the long term you need to examine your lifestyle and make the necessary changes suggested under "controllable risk factors" (see pages 777).

What your physician can do. Your physician can thoroughly evaluate your condition, both by a physical examination and by making a number of laboratory tests. These may include blood pressure, an electrocardiogram, blood tests to determine the level of your fats (triglycerides) and cholesterol, a chest X-ray to show the size of your heart, and an angiogram (by the injection of a dye) to estimate the blood flow through your coronary arteries.

Heart attack

A heart attack occurs when blood flow through one of the coronary arteries or its major branches is blocked by a thrombus or blood clot, due usually to advanced atherosclerosis. The area of heart muscle damaged by lack of blood is called an **infarct.** If the infarct is small and the conducting system of the heart is not affected, the chance of recovery is good. The attack may occur suddenly and without warning, or it may come on gradually.

The pain from a heart attack may parallel that experienced with severe angina (see page 782), but generally it is not relieved by rest or the elimination of the emotional stress that triggered it, and frequently will last for thirty or more minutes. The pain may vary

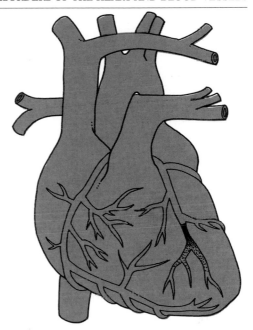

Note that a blood clot in the anterior branch of the left coronary artery has deprived the muscle of the heart wall of blood (mottled area). This is what happens in a heart attack.

widely, from agonizing to mild, with various combinations of symptoms. Usually the intense pain originates in the chest, with a crushing, squeezing feeling. The victim may experience sweating, cold, clammy skin, nausea, vomiting, weakness, shortness of breath, dizziness and fainting, and a feeling of impending death.

In the Western world heart attacks are the most common cause of death, one in three being fatal. The care given in the first few minutes may make the difference between life and death, so don't delay in getting medical help. The American Medical Association gives some good advice: "Don't you wait. If you think someone is having a heart attack, call the fire department rescue squad immediately. Seconds count. Don't wait for severe pain, dizziness, fainting or sweating, or shortness of breath. . . . Don't let the fear of embarrassment delay your call. If you're wrong about the existence of a heart attack, it doesn't matter. If you're right, nothing could matter more." So any unexplained chest pain which persists for more than a few minutes should be examined by a physician.

What you can do. A heart attack is an emergency. If you are with someone who experiences severe chest pains, call for professional help: a physician, fire department rescue squad, or ambulance. Place the victim in a half-reclining position with head and shoulders slightly elevated. You may save a life if you or someone at hand can administer cardiopulmonary resuscitation (CPR)—mouth-to-mouth breathing with external heart massage—so oxygen can reach the brain and vital areas. Allow the victim to breathe fresh air. If oxygen is available, play a gentle stream over the face and nose. A nitroglycerine tablet, if available, can be placed under the tongue. The sooner the victim reaches a hospital or coronary-care unit, the better.

What your physician can do. While bed rest initially is mandatory, your physician will assess the severity of the attack and allow as much activity as he deems wise, since bed rest may increase the risk of abnormal clotting. He may order a platelet (thrombocyte) count and prescribe an anticoagulant to further reduce the risk of a blood clot forming, and

he will relieve pain when necessary. Oxygen may make breathing easier. He will order a number of tests, such as electrocardiograms (EKG), to monitor the type and extent of the injury and blood tests to measure the damage done to the heart muscle. If

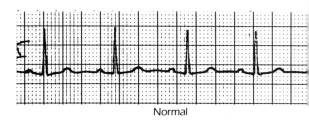

Normal

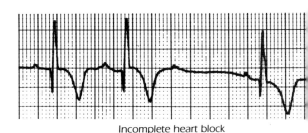

Incomplete heart block

Typical electrocardiogram (EKG) tracings, showing normal and irregular heart action.

the heart begins to fail or the heart rhythms are disturbed, he may prescribe other medications.

The long-term prospects depend on the extent of the damage and on the steps taken to actively modify all risk factors present in the lifestyle. In case of mild heart attack, without complications, full recovery can be expected. If severe, some loss of functional activity may result. Lifestyle modifications, which include stopping smoking, exercise, weight loss, dietary changes, and restyling of behavior, together with long-term medical follow-up, will largely determine the outcome.

Because many heart problems result from atherosclerosis, and the procedures of rehabilitation, coronary bypass surgery, and angioplasty apply to more than one problem, the details are presented at the end of this section (see page 790).

Hypertension

Because it affects the heart so frequently, hypertension or high blood pressure is discussed here rather than under vascular diseases. High blood pressure is the most common and dangerous underlying cause of heart and blood vessel disease, and it is the leading cause of death in industrialized nations. Hypertension, called the "silent killer," produces no symptoms during the first fifteen or so years and goes undetected without blood pressure measurements. Only in advanced stages, and not always then, will symptoms appear—headache, nosebleed, dizziness, fainting, and ringing of the ears. But despite the fact that no symptoms appear, high blood pressure silently, slowly, but surely, injures the heart, damages the arteries (especially those of the heart, brain, eyes, and kidneys), and cuts short the lifespan by ten to twenty years.

What is blood pressure? Blood pressure is the force required by the heart to pump blood against the resistance offered by the arteries. The arteries are always full of blood. Their walls consist of layers of muscle and elastic tissue, so they can expand and contract. When the heart contracts, it pushes 4 to 8 ounces of blood into already full vessels. The arteries must bulge outward to accept the heart's output, and then their musculo-elastic walls recoil, maintaining pressure to continue the flow. When the heart contracts, systolic pressure is highest; when the heart relaxes, diastolic pressure is the lowest. The normal range for blood pressure in healthy young adults is 90 to 140 for the systolic and 60 to 90 for the diastolic.

What is high blood pressure? Persistent readings above 160 systolic or above 95 diastolic fall into the range of high blood pressure. Notice the words *persistent readings* above these figures. A single reading may not indicate your average blood pressure. Blood pressure may abruptly rise under stress, excitement, or an emergency, but should drop back to normal when the cause is removed.

The cause of hypertension in the overwhelming majority of cases is idiopathic or of unknown cause. Secondary hypertension may result from chronic kidney disease, certain hormonal disorders, and, in certain women, becoming pregnant or taking oral contraceptives.

A certain form of hypertension (essential hypertension) has no known cause, though research suggests one possibility—that a gradual increase in the volume of blood accompanies a slow rise in blood pressure. Some inherited inability of the kidneys to excrete excess salt in the diet causes this increase in blood volume. This would explain why hypertension

785

seems to run in families. The child of a parent with high blood pressure has twice the chance of developing hypertension as a child whose parents have normal blood pressure. Another observation is that overweight children seem more likely to have hypertension when they reach middle age than normal-weight children.

Undiscovered or uncontrolled hypertension can be a deadly disease. The increased pressure within the arteries accelerates the process of atherosclerosis in the coronary arteries, and in the arteries of the brain, kidneys, and other organs. The result is more than a twofold increase in heart attacks and sudden death, a sixfold increase in conges-

What you can do. As already mentioned, hypertension can be considered a symptomless disease. Should you discover you have the problem, you can reduce your salt intake, if it is high; you can lose weight, if you are obese. If you smoke, give it up because smoking contributes to atherosclerosis and heart disease. If you are a type A person on a tight schedule, reduce your emotional stress; include regular exercise in your program because exercise is relaxing; and seek help from your physician.

What your physician can do. Even mild high blood pressure is harmful over time. If your own efforts fail to reduce your blood pressure, a number of medications are

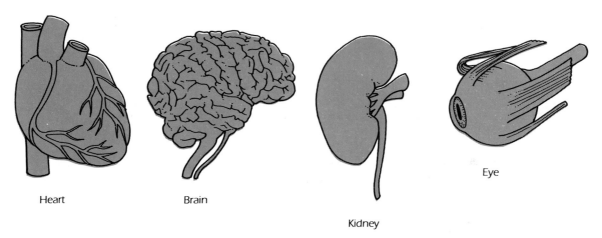

Heart   Brain

Eye

Kidney

Untreated high blood pressure accelerates the process of atherosclerosis in the arteries of the heart,

brain, kidneys, and eye, resulting in heart attacks, stroke, kidney failure, and retinal (eye) problems.

tive heart failure, a fourfold increase in strokes, and a two-fold increase from fatal kidney disease in hypertensives as compared with those having normal blood pressure.

available. These must be taken under the guidance of your physician, who will determine which are most effective. Diuretics or "water pills" reduce the amount of salt and water in your constantly think about how you are standing and sitting.

The secret to good posture is to learn to flatten your pelvis, because this determines the forward and backward curvatures of your spine. To accomplish this, contract your large gluteal muscles (those of your buttocks) while standing. This throws your pubis upward. You cannot do this while walking, but practice it whenever you are standing. Then stand and sit tall, holding your head erect with your chin out. Allow your arms to hang naturally by your sides. If you have developed rounded shoulders, you may have to pull them backwards for a period of time.

Good posture is a real asset. It will improve your health and appearance. It will give you poise and grace. It will provide you with a positive influence and make you more readily accepted by others. You will look and feel better.

Disorders of muscles

Muscle cramps

Muscle cramps occur when muscles in certain localized areas go into violent spasm, most commonly seen in the muscles of the calf, back of the thigh, and feet. While the precise cause has not, as yet, been determined, certain factors appear to precipitate their occurrence. These include severe cold, poor circulation to the affected area, overexercise of the muscle, stretching the muscle too much, pointing the toes forward (extending the foot), and dehydration (lack of sufficient water intake).

Night cramps frequently wake some people up with extreme pain. However, the condition is harmless. Something in the muscle (lack of oxygen, excess lactic acid, faulty relaxation) triggers a reflex response from the spinal cord. This contraction, in turn, further stimulates the sensory nerves, causing another response from the cord, which increases the spasm.

Swimmer's cramp is similar to the cramp discussed above. It occurs more frequently among swimmers who kick with their feet stretched out (extended). Avoid overextending your feet while swimming. Some of the procedures described below may be helpful.

What you can do. Once the cramp has occurred it will relax of its own accord. However, to hasten its relaxation, try contracting the muscles that produce a movement in a direction opposite to that which the cramping muscles are pulling. For instance, if your calf muscles are in spasm and drawing your foot downward, hold the foot in that position while trying to draw the foot upwards (towards your shin). This may provide immediate relief. Do not stretch the cramped muscle too far. Another suggestion: stand on the balls of your feet while raising and lowering your heels.

Some people obtain relief by gently massaging the affected muscles.

963

Raising the foot of the bed helps others. A warm footbath, which increases the circulation in the legs and feet, will also give relief, and if taken before going to bed will frequently prevent their occurrence. Heavy bed clothes which force the foot forward (toward the sole) may precipitate an attack. Try using a cradle or pillow under the covers to remove the weight of the covers from the feet. Drink plenty of water, especially during hard physical exercise and especially in hot weather.

A simple exercise done during the day may also help. Stand erect in stocking feet. Lean forward, keeping your heels on the floor until you feel a pulling sensation in the calf muscles. Hold for ten seconds, then repeat after a five-second interval of rest. Do this five times, two or three times a day, until the night cramps disappear.

What your physician can do. Should the above measures fail to bring relief, have your physician determine if there is some underlying cause for the problem. Quinine (a toxic drug used to treat malaria) for some unknown reason gives relief. However, it should only be used on your physician's advice.

Claudication is pain and spasm that occurs most commonly in the muscles of the calf, and is brought on by walking. It results from an inadequate blood supply to the cramping muscles. The cramps may be triggered by vigorous exercise beyond that for which your muscles are conditioned or from advancing atherosclerosis, which is gradually reducing the flow of blood through your arteries.

What you can do. Rest will promptly relieve the spasm and pain. If your problem is one of inactivity, go on a regular exercise program. Should you suspect atherosclerosis, consult with your physician. He will evaluate the underlying cause and advise an exercise program, hot-and-cold contrast baths, or a medication which will increase circulation in the area.

Wryneck (torticollis)

Wryneck, a spasm of the muscles on one side of the neck, twists the neck and draws the head over in an unnatural position to that side.

The causes may include a temporary contraction of the muscles due to exposure to cold, to an injury, to enlargement of the lymph glands of the neck (from infection in the neck or pharynx), to local irritation of the muscles, or to emotional problems. It may result from a congenital disorder in which the muscles of one side of the neck shorten and become fibrous or the skin of one side of the neck contracts.

What you can do. In mild cases, apply heat (moist or dry), massage the area gently, and stretch it five times a day. This may relieve the situation. If the problem does not respond to this treatment in two or three days, see your physician.

What your physician can do. He can determine and treat the underlying cause. Wryneck, observed early in infancy, may require surgical intervention to release the contracted muscles, and then a splint or cast to hold the head in proper position for a period of time.

Myofascitis (myofascial pain, fibrositis)

In **myofascitis,** stiffness, aching, and deep pain occur in certain parts of the body. The neck, the shoulders, the lower back, and the thighs are the areas most often affected. The sufferer complains of stiff neck, pain in the thigh, or arthritis, all worse in the morning, and often with tender swellings or "knots" in the muscles. The cause of this discomfort, which generally occurs in those forty to sixty years of age and is sometimes associated with inability to sleep, is unknown.

What you can do. The condition is not serious and lasts from a few hours to a week or two. Rest, together with heat applications (hot baths, heating pad, heat lamp, or fomentations) and gentle massage will bring relief. If the discomfort persists, see your physician.

What your physician can do. He may prescribe a muscle relaxant and something to relieve pain. Injections of a steroid into the tender, painful areas are often helpful.

Muscular dystrophy

Muscular dystrophy comprises a group of congenital disorders showing progressive weakness and wasting of the muscles. The most common form, **Duchenne dystrophy,** appears only in male infants or very young boys. The weakness starts in the muscles of the hips, thighs, and calves, and may progress to the shoulders and elsewhere in the body. The child walks with a waddling gait, falls frequently, and has difficulty in standing up again. There is no known treatment, and the illness is progressively unfavorable.

Juvenile dystrophy usually begins during adolescence and affects both sexes equally. The weakness often starts in the shoulders and then affects the face and upper arms. Eventually the muscles in the hands, feet, and back become involved. The back becomes swayed, and the arms and legs are held in abnormal positions. The disease may become arrested spontaneously.

What your physician can do. Laboratory tests, including a biopsy of a muscle, will determine the precise diagnosis. Genetic counseling should be sought as to the risks involved in marriage and having additional children. The physician will direct treatment toward maintaining as much functional activity as long as possible. Physical therapy and surgery to correct deformities may prove helpful.

Polymyositis and dermatomyositis. See under "collagen diseases," page 957.

Skin and hair

The skin covers the entire surface of your body, an area of more than 18 square feet, and weighs twice as much as your heart or liver—approximately 10 pounds (4.5 kilograms). An area of skin the size of a postage stamp (2.2 x 3.6 centimeters) is made up of more than 25 million cells, containing approximately 560 sweat glands, 90 oil (sebaceous) glands, and 60 hairs, with thousands of sensory nerve receptors for touch, pain, cold, heat, and pressure. Besides these, there are numerous muscles and yards (meters) of nerves and blood vessels.

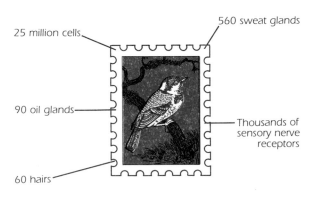

25 million cells

560 sweat glands

90 oil glands

60 hairs

Thousands of sensory nerve receptors

Note the many structures in a piece of skin the size of this stamp.

The skin is what you first see of others, and what they first see of you. Soft, smooth, and elastic, it adds beauty and color to the form and contours of your body. But it differs in thickness and design in various areas of the body, depending on its functional needs. It is paper thin on the eyelids, but strong and thick on the palms of the hands and soles of the feet. It is an organ of many purposes.

The skin consists of three parts: the epidermis on the outside, the dermis beneath the epidermis, with the subcutaneous tissue deep to both.

The **epidermis** contains no blood vessels—but layer upon layer of cells. Nourished by tissue fluid, its deepest cells are alive and constantly produce more cells like themselves. The new cells are pushed toward the surface, and thus are gradually removed from their source of nourishment. As they die, they undergo a chemical change to form keratin, a horny material that is tough, insensitive, and impermeable to water. Eventually, as they reach the surface, they are rubbed off. As fast as surface cells are lost, new cells form so that the skin is virtually indestructible.

This epidermal layer of skin protects the body from outside assault: from physical injury, for the skin is tough even though it is soft, resilient, and pliable; from chemical attack, for while the skin can absorb many chemicals, it blocks the penetration of most and retards the entry of others; and from germs, both bacteria and fungi, for the human skin is covered with an acid coat that hampers the growth of these microorganisms. The skin also protects the body's inner environment, for without it, vital body fluids, containing life-preserving substances, would soon be lost.

The **dermis** is a mat of strong interlacing fibers containing blood vessels, lymph channels, nerves, muscles, sweat and sebaceous glands, hair follicles, and a vast array of sense organs, which give us the sensations of hot and cold and the feeling of touch, pain, and pressure. Furthermore, the skin can repair itself following injury.

Just beneath the dermis is a layer of **subcutaneous tissue,** a loose network of fibers (connective tissue) with an abundance of fat cells. This layer of subcutaneous fat is thicker in women than in men, deeper in some places than others, and fills in the hollows between the deeper structures, giving the skin a smooth and beautiful appearance. This layer of fat provides protection from injury, insulation from the entry of cold or the escape of body heat, and serves as a depository of fuel, a store of energy for time of need. These fat stores increase when you put on weight.

The amount of melanin, a pigment

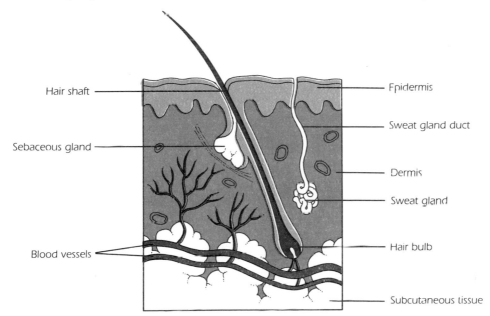

The layers of the skin and its many structures.

produced by some 5 percent of the cells in the epidermis, and the amount of blood momentarily present in the dermis determine the color of the skin. The more melanin present, the darker the complexion. The rosy complexion seen in fair-skinned people is due to a greater flow of blood in the dermal layer. And interestingly, the skin can reveal the state of your emotions: pale and bumpy (goose pimples) when afraid, red when angry, flushed or blushed when ashamed, and wet with sweat when stressed.

The skin's **sweat glands,** shaped like tiny coiled tubes, extract water and salt from the blood capillaries and secrete them on the skin's surface. A large and different type of sweat gland found in the armpit and groin secretes a sweat which develops a distinctive odor. The majority of the **sebaceous** or **oil glands** are located adjacent to the hair follicles and produce an oily substance (sebum) that keeps the skin pliable and the hairs from becoming dry. Drying sweat mixed with sebum collects dust and dirt, and becomes offensive. This is an excellent reason for washing and bathing.

The skin of a child is soft and smooth, but gradually changes with age. During adolescence the oil glands become more active, especially on the face. The skin may appear greasy, and blackheads and pimples tend to develop (see page 983). With maturity the secretion of oil slows down, and with advancing age, oil production further decreases. The skin becomes less elastic, which largely accounts for the appearance

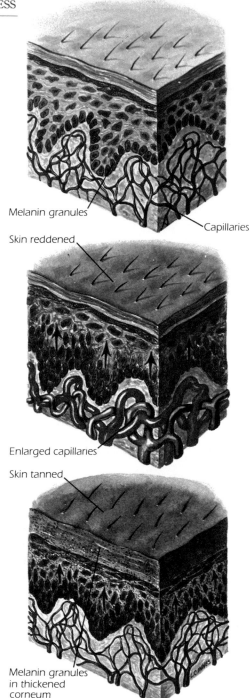

Melanin granules

Capillaries

Skin reddened

Enlarged capillaries

Skin tanned

Melanin granules in thickened corneum

Effects of exposure of skin to sunlight: upper, normal skin; middle, twenty-four hours after exposure (redness from blood-filled capillaries); lower, one week after exposure (tan coloration due to increase in granules of melanin).

of wrinkles. Drying, wrinkling, and aging of the skin can be delayed by avoiding too much exposure to sunlight and wind, and from smoking cigarettes.

The surface of the dermis is not a straight plane but undulates with ridges and valleys. These, in turn, fit into corresponding valleys and ridges on the undersurface of the epidermis and are reflected on the surface of the skin. These ridges and valleys seen on the tips of your fingers and toes, when pressed on a smooth surface, leave behind **fingerprints** (and toeprints), each with a particular pattern, unique for each individual. This unevenness of the skin on the hands and feet allows a person to grip objects more surely and walk more securely.

The skin contains millions of **sense organs** located on the undersurface of the epidermis. These include the receptors for pain, touch, heat, cold, and pressure. There is approximately one pain receptor for every square millimeter of skin, or the size of this *o*. The number varies, however, depending on the area of the skin, being less numerous on the back than on the fingertips. This is also true of touch. Almost twenty-five times as many tactile bodies occur on the tips of the fingers and toes as on the back.

Our skin sensors not only tell us that something is cold or warn us when something is hot, but also help us to maintain a remarkably constant **temperature,** regardless of our environment. When the body tends to overheat, blood is rushed to the skin, where heat is dissipated, aided by the evaporation of sweat. To reduce the radiation of heat from the body when exposed to cold, the blood vessels in the skin constrict, sweat production ceases, and the oil glands pour out more oil, which spreads on the skin and further reduces evaporation.

Tattooing involves injecting an insoluble dye (black or colored) into the dermis. Once the dye is placed, it is extremely difficult to remove without leaving a scar. Another serious problem is the danger of contracting an infection, such as AIDS or hepatitis, from a needle that was not properly sterilized.

When a large area of skin has been destroyed by a burn or injury, to hasten healing and to prevent scarring, a surgeon may make a **skin graft.** Generally a split-thickness graft is used, in which a thin layer of skin is shaved off some other area, such as the abdomen, back, or thigh and bandaged in place on the denuded area until attached. Sometimes a pedicle graft is necessary, in which a piece of skin close at hand is partially removed and stretched over the destroyed area. More recently, grafts taken from neonatal (newborn) foreskin and autographs (a person's own skin) grown in culture are being used to replace the dstroyed skin.

Fingernails and **hairs,** produced by cells of the epidermis **(keratinocytes),** are keratin structures similar to the cells on the skin's surface. Nails are produced by cells that proliferate at the base or matrix of the nail, while hairs are made by similar cells reproducing in hair follicles.

The process parallels that which takes place in the epidermis. As new cells form in the nail matrix or hair follicle, they are pushed toward the surface, become removed from their source of nourishment, die, and become hardened keratin.

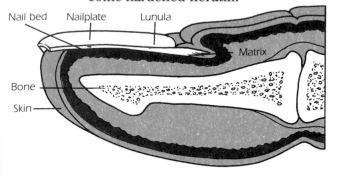

A section showing the major structures of the nail.

Within the hair follicle are pigment-producing cells which intermingle with the hair cells. As the pigment cells die, they leave their pigment granules behind, giving color to the hair. The loss of this pigment is responsible for the graying of hair. This pigment is also responsible for the repigmentation of a person with vitiligo. Because the nail matrix has no pigment-producing cells, nails are clear colored.

It is estimated that a person has from one-third to half a million hairs on the skin. Fair-haired people have more and finer hairs. Hairs on the beards of men, scalp, eyebrow, and pubis grow longer than do those elsewhere on the body.

CHAPTER 15

Diseases of the skin, nails, and hair

Skin diseases affect all age groups. While many similarities exist among the various skin disorders, important differences often point to the specific cause and indicate the best treatment.

Dermatitis

Dermatitis, frequently referred to as eczema, is an inflammation of the skin. Such disorders may result from an inborn sensitivity (inherited), acquired sensitivity, exposure to some agent, or to emotional stress. Thus skin diseases have many causes and take many forms. Only the more familiar will be discussed.

The common characteristics of dermatitis are reddening, swelling, blistering, oozing, crusting, and itching. Depending on the condition, there may also be scaling and changes in the color or pigments of the skin.

Atopic dermatitis

This condition is an inflammation of the skin resulting from an inherited hypersensitivity. Seventy-five percent of sufferers have relatives who are troubled with asthma, hay fever, and hives. While it may occur at any age, it is most likely to occur during infancy and childhood.

The disorder varies in intensity from time to time. In infants it affects the face and outer surfaces of the arms and legs. In children it usually affects the skin on the inner surface of the arms and legs. From adolescence onward the lesions tend to be more dry with the formation of plaques, especially in the skinfolds of the arms and legs, on the neck, face, hands, and in the crotch. At all ages scratching further aggravates the situation. The problem tends to become less severe as one gets older.

A number of factors may provoke or intensify atopic dermatitis. These include marked changes in tempera-

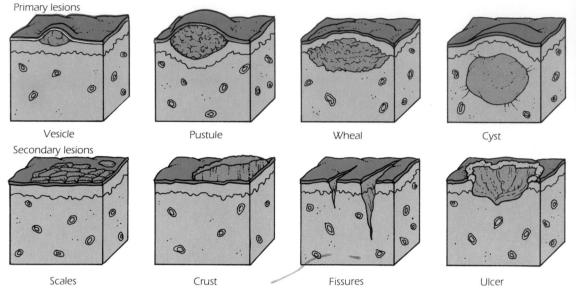

Primary lesions

Vesicle   Pustule   Wheal   Cyst

Secondary lesions

Scales   Crust   Fissures   Ulcer

Common lesions of the skin.

ture (cold weather, heat and humidity), profuse sweating (from vigorous physical activity), exposure to certain chemicals (grease, solvents, detergents), excessive clothing (especially woolen and coarse-textured garments), psychological stress, and allergens. In general, food allergies and pollens carried in the air are not related to the disorder.

What you can do. Since there is no cure, you must try to avoid anything which will trigger an episode, while treatment is directed toward relieving the symptoms. Itching causes scratching, and scratching intensifies the itching, aggravates the lesions, and encourages infections. Wet dressings help to clean the lesions and reduce itching while the eczema is wet and oozing. Bathing and soap may intensify the problem. Cleansing creams may be used instead. Constant lubrication with a soothing cream or ointment is a necessity. When washing clothes and

bed sheets, avoid detergents, use a mild soap, and thoroughly rinse the wash.

What your physician can do. He will instruct you how to cleanse and care for your lesions. Cortisone ointments as well as purified tar preparations with cautious ultraviolet light exposure will reduce both the itching and the inflammation. In severe cases oral antihistamines and steroids may sometimes be recommended. An appropriate antibiotic will control a secondary infection.

Contact dermatitis

Contact dermatitis, as the name suggests, is an acute inflammatory eruption resulting from direct contact with an irritant material or to some substance to which an acquired sensitivity (allergy) has developed.

Irritant dermatitis can occur from a number of commonly used agents which include detergents, bleaches, toilet bowl cleaners, strong alkalis and acids, furniture polishes, aerosols, swimming pool disinfectants, adhesive bandages, rubber gloves, elastic components in stretch garments, and industrial solvents and oils.

Allergic dermatitis results from a sensitivity to a substance developed from a previous exposure to it. Almost 75 percent of the population react to contact with **poison ivy** and **poison oak.** One can acquire sensitivity to almost any substance: the dyes in leather, the elastic in garments, fingernail polishes, and to metals in jewelry, such as nickel.

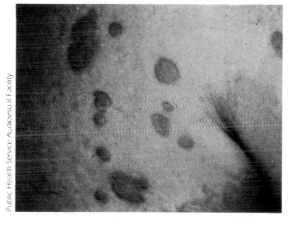

Public Health Service Audiovisual Facility

Rash caused from administration of penicillin.

Dermatitis from irritants causes reddening, blistering, drying, and cracking. Painful fissures and ulcers may develop. Itching, if present, is mild. In response to a substance to which you have become sensitive, the skin becomes red, and small to large blisters form. These break to ooze and weep. The eyes and face may be puffy. Itching may be intense. As healing occurs, the lesions will dry and crust. Allergies to metals develop slowly and cause itching, scaling, and redness.

What you can do. Try to avoid contact with any substance to which you respond adversely. To determine whether you will react to a substance, try a patch test. Put a drop or a tiny amount of the material on a very small piece of gauze, place it in contact with the skin of your abdomen or inner thigh, cover the gauze with wax paper, and attach it with a piece of adhesive tape. Leave it in place for forty-eight hours unless itching and irritation occur earlier, at which point it should be removed. If you have no reaction, the substance is likely safe for you to use.

Your physician may be able to do sensitivity tests for things to which you have become allergic. Careful observation on your part as to the circumstances under which you develop dermatitis will greatly aid him in recognizing the offending materials.

For irritant dermatitis, protect yourself from exposure. Wear cotton gloves inside rubber gloves when doing dishes or other chores in which your hands might come in contact with an irritant. Should you become exposed, wash the material off as quickly as possible. For exposure to poison oak or ivy, use soap to remove the waxy or resinous toxic material, and thoroughly wash all clothes involved.

Many of the procedures for treating contact dermititis are similar to those discussed under atopic dermatitis. Wet dressings, mild ointments, and calamine lotion should reduce itching and bring relief.

973

What your physician can do. He can test for agents to which you might have become sensitive. Depending on the severity of the inflammation, steroid ointments and antihistamines may be recommended. An appropriate antibiotic will care for a secondary infection.

Other inflammatory skin disorders

A number of inflammatory skin disorders similar to atopic and contact dermatitis, but which do have certain differences, are briefly presented.

Seborrheic dermatitis is a common condition in which thick, yellowish, greasy (sometimes dry) scales affect the scalp **(dandruff),** the sides of the nose, corners of the mouth, and the crease behind the ears. Often the eyelids and lid margins become red and scaly **(blepharitis).** More severe cases involve the face and neck, and the armpits, groin, and genital regions **(intertrigo).** It may come and go, or persist for years. While the cause is unknown, there appears to be a hereditary tendency.

Certain shampoos are quite effective in controlling scalp problems. Low-dosage cortisone-containing lotions, creams, and ointments give effective relief. See your physician before using cortisone-containing preparations for prolonged periods or around the eyes, as damage to the skin and eyes may occur. Should intertriginous seborrhea become infected, wet dressings, and antibiotic or antifungal agents used topically or systemically, are helpful.

Chronic dermatitis, similar to atopic dermatitis but more localized, may appear in any age group. Itching is intense, and the skin thickens through constant scratching. Chronic dermatitis commonly affects the shins, ankles, inner thighs, and the cleft between the legs, neck, and forearms. Frequently the cause of the itching is not known. Protecting the affected areas from scratching, together with a steroid ointment and antihistamines, often brings relief.

Xerotic eczema is a dry, scaling irritation of the skin, seen especially on the lower legs in the elderly. Severity increases in dry weather and improves as the humidity rises. Moistening of the skin with soothing lotions and bath oils, and bathing less frequently and without detergent soaps, provide relief. When the air is dry, a humidifier may be beneficial.

Dyshidrosis is an inflammatory eruption occurring along the sides of the fingers, on the palms of the hands, and on the soles of the feet. It produces mild itching and burning. Small blisters form which break and ooze, or dry up and turn brown. The skin may peel later. The cause is not known; however, it may be related to atopic dermatitis in adulthood. The disorder goes in cycles, may be induced by stress, and is worsened with increased exposure to water. A subtype, "housewife's eczema" ("dishpan hands"), occurs in those whose hands are frequently exposed to the chemicals listed under contact dermatitis. The skin becomes red, chapped, dry, cracked, and fissured. Small to large blisters may develop, which break and weep. For treatment, see under "contact dermititis," page 972.

Stasis dermatitis

This disorder shows red, scaly patches of skin on the front and inner side of the lower leg and ankle. It may or may not itch and results from failure of the circulation in the veins. The skin may break down and an ulcer form. Stasis dermatitis is often associated with varicose veins or thrombophlebitis.

What you can do. Avoid standing for long periods of time. Do not cross one thigh over the other. When seated, try to elevate your feet to the level of your hips. In stubborn cases, elevating the foot of your bed about four inches may help improve veinous circulation. If you have prominent leg veins, wear support hose or an elastic bandage to decrease stagnation of blood in the veins.

Walking will improve the circulation in your legs. Be careful not to injure the lower leg. Should your problem persist and these simple treatments prove ineffective, see your physician.

Nummular dermatitis

This eczema appears as round, coin-shaped lesions (*nummulus* means "coin"), mostly seen on the extremities of older men and young adult women. It may develop as a single lesion or several lesions that may recur in episodes. The cause is unknown but may be related to a bacterial infection and dry weather. The condition may worsen with contact with wool, soaps, medications applied to the skin, and frequent bathing.

What you can do. When bathing, hydrate the skin by using oil additives. Keep the skin from drying by the generous use of body creams.

What your physician can do. He can prescribe an appropriate coal tar preparation or a topical steroid.

Bacterial infections of the skin

Bacterial infections may be caused by a variety of organisms, but the most common are staphylococcus and streptococcus. The infections are usually contagious. The lesions become red, blister, create pus, and form a crust. The neighboring lymph glands may be tender and swollen. Some people develop fever and general illness. Treatment is appropriate antibiotics.

Impetigo

Impetigo, a common, acute, contagious, superficial skin infection occurring in adults but most often in children, is usually caused by staphylococci or by streptococci. The lesions ordinarily appear around the mouth and nose. If caused by streptococci, small red blisters break and fuse, forming pustules that ooze. As they dry, loosely attached golden-yellow or honey-colored crusts form in one to two days. The infection spreads along the margins, is itchy but not painful, and generally disappears by itself in two to three weeks. If caused by staphylococci, small blisters form that easily break, leaving a denuded base.

The disease is seldom dangerous, except in infants, where it can become widespread, and if streptococci are involved, may cause a serious kidney disease (glomerulonephritis).

What you can do. Keep your fingers away from the crusts and do not scratch them, as this tends to spread the infection. Your face cloths, towels, and linens should not be shared by other family members. Children with this disorder should be kept out of school. Gently wash the lesions with soap and water. However, because of possible complications, you should see your physician.

What your physician can do. He will probably recommend an anti-infective ointment to rub on the lesions after washing. An antibiotic by mouth or injection is effective, and the condition should clear up in about a week.

Folliculitis

Folliculitis is a superficial infection of one or more hair follicles, usually caused by staphylococcus bacteria. The follicle becomes red, fills with pus, forms crusts, spreads to adjacent follicles, and most commonly affects the bearded area of men or any hair-bearing skin. Young bearded adults can suffer from chronic recurrent folliculitis.

What you can do. The treatment is similar to that for impetigo: gentle cleaning of the infected area with an antibacterial soap, the nonsharing of towels and linens, the use of an antibacterial ointment following shaving, and, when necessary, an antibiotic by mouth provided by your physician.

Boils (furuncles)

A boil is a hard, red, very painful infection affecting a localized group of hair follicles (a complication of folliculitis), that is caused by staphylococcus bacteria. It commonly develops under the arms, on the face, on the scalp, on the inner sides of the thighs, and on the buttocks. As the boil enlarges, a core forms, the surface skin softens and then ruptures, allowing the pus within to escape. A boil that develops on the eyelid is called a sty.

Avoid the dangerous practice of

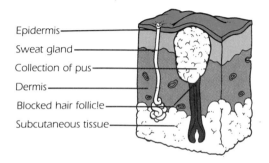

Epidermis
Sweat gland
Collection of pus
Dermis
Blocked hair follicle
Subcutaneous tissue

Boil resulting from an infected hair follicle.

picking or squeezing a boil (or pimple), as this may force the germs into surrounding tissues or into the bloodstream (septicemia). This is especially true of boils forming in the area between the nose, upper lip, cheek, and eyebrow, and inside the nostril, as the infection may travel to the brain.

When a number of boils develop in the deep layers of the skin adjacent to one another, the lesion is called a **carbuncle.** Often accompanied with fever, carbuncles have multiple heads and are commonly seen on the back of the neck, back, and thighs.

976

What you can do. The same principles of treatment apply to boils as to folliculitis. Warm, moist compresses (several layers of gauze wrung out of hot water) applied several times a day will hasten the boil's coming to a "head" and discharging its contents.

What your physician can do. Your physician may choose to open (lance) the boil rather than allowing it to rupture by itself. Should the boil persist, he may prescribe a suitable antibiotic. He will also determine if some underlying problem, such as diabetes, obesity, or anemia may be a contributing factor.

Cellulitis

Cellulitis, a serious infection affecting the tissues beneath the skin as well as the skin itself, is usually caused by staphylococcal or streptococcal bacteria which gain entrance through a break in the skin. The infection spreads along the lymph channels, causing red streaks in the direction of the lymph nodes that service the area. The nodes become enlarged and tender, while the affected skin is hot, red, and painful. The sufferer feels ill and has chills, fever, and headache.

Erysipelas, sometimes considered a form of cellulitis, is also a serious infection caused by streptococcus bacteria occurring in the more superficial skin layers. The affected area, frequently the face, reddens and swells, spreads in all directions, and itches and burns. The firm margins of the infection are easily felt (in contrast to cellulitis), and, if on the face, stop abruptly at the hairline. The general symptoms are the same as for cellulitis.

What your physician can do. If untreated, cellulitis, and especially erysipelas, can be fatal, as the organisms may enter the bloodstream, causing septicemia (blood poisoning). Effective antibiotics are available to treat these infections. Hot compresses may give local relief.

Fungal infections of the skin

Fungal infections tend to be persistent, but seldom form true pus or cause fever. Fungi are more complex than bacteria and multiply by means of spores. In general these infections do not respond to antibiotics. Some are extremely common, and most people have at least one fungal infection. The most common conditions are ringworm infections (dermatophytosis), yeast infections (candidiasis), and tinea versicolor (changing color).

Ringworm infections (dermatophytosis)

Ringworm infections (tinea) are not caused by a worm as the name would suggest, but by fungi. The term *ringworm* stems from the observation that the lesions tend to heal at their centers and continue to spread in a widening, ringlike fashion. Although these infections are spread by contact with people and pet animals, or by contact with infected objects used by others (towels, combs, etc.)

the affected person probably has an inherited inability to combat a particular fungus. This is the reason why, in a camp or family, only certain people develop the disease.

Athlete's foot (tinea pedis)

This infection is a form of ringworm occurring between the toes in which the skin softens, turns white, and tends to peel and flake. Blisters and cracks appear. Secondary infection is common, resulting in the formation of ulcers and pus with itching and burning. Probably the most common infection of the skin, it is quite contagious and is spread from contaminated shoes, showers (especially public), and areas surrounding swimming pools. The hands may be affected in two ways: (1) Painless "blisters" develop on both hands as an allergic response to toxins produced by the infection in the feet (carried in the blood to the hands—dermatophytid reaction). (2) Scaling of one hand (2 feet, 1 hand disease), which is also affected by the fungus.

What you can do. Wash your feet daily (or more often), dry thoroughly between the toes, use an antifungal powder (antifungal creams tend to keep the skin moist), use absorbent socks, and, whenever possible, wear sandals and air your feet. Should the problem continue, see your physician for systemic medicine.

Ringworm of the scalp, body, and groin (tinea capitis, t. corporis, t. cruris)

Ringworm of the scalp—most common in children—presents small, round, reddish, scaly spots with blisters. The spots enlarge rapidly, become grayish in color, and show definite boundaries. The affected hair shafts break off, and patchy hair loss results. If this persistent inflammation is left untreated, permanent hair loss may result.

Ringworm of the body may affect all areas of the skin except the scalp and groin. It first appears as pea-sized reddened patches, which, while growing rapidly, heal in the center, thus forming rings. The outer edges show tiny papules and small blisters. There is mild itching.

Ringworm of the groin (jock or crotch itch) presents brownish-red scaly patches with tiny blisters at the spreading edges. There is mild itching and smarting. It affects the inner surfaces of the upper thighs and the genital and anal areas. Heat, moisture, profuse sweating, and chafing by clothing aggravate the infection. This disorder is seen more frequently in men.

Ringworm of the beard (barber's itch) is an inflammation in and around the hair follicles. Superficial nodules appear in groups, become deep-seated, discharge a thin pus, itch, and are mildly painful.

Ringworm of the nails affects either fingernails or toenails, which become thickened, brittle, broken, white, and often ridged. Frequently only one nail is affected.

What your physician can do. After an appropriate diagnosis, your physician will prescribe an ointment containing a fungicide, or an oral antibiotic (griseofulvin is commonly used, as it is secreted through the

Asbestosis, 3-930
Ascariasis
    See Roundworms
Ascites, 2-613
Aspirin, 1-330
    Cautions concerning use of, 1-331, 2-467, 2-732
Asthma, 3-920
    In children, 2-458, 2-470
Asthma attack, 2-529
Astigmatism, 3-1187
Atherosclerosis, 1-7, 3-776, 3-779
    Angioplasty as treatment for, 3-790
    Atheroma (plaque), 3-780
    See also Arteries: arteriosclerosis
    In children, 2-457
    Increased risk of, in diabetes, 3-1014
    Plaque (atheroma), 3-780
    Risk factors in, 3-776, 3-777
    Symptoms of, 3-780
Athlete's foot (tinea pedia), 3-978
Attention deficit disorder
    See Hyperactive child
Autonomic nervous system
    See Involuntary nervous system
AZT (azidothymidine) as AIDS treatment, 3-831
Azul
    See Pinto

B

Baby teeth
    See Teeth, Primary (deciduous)
Bacillary dysentery (shigellosis), 2-712
Back pain, 2-642
Bacteremia, 2-703
Bacterial endocarditis
    See Endocarditis
Bacterial infection, 3-705
Bad breath
    See Halitosis
"Bag of waters," 2-399
Balantidial dysentery (balantidiasis), 2-745
Balantidiasis
    See balantidial dysentery
Baldness, 3-992
    Alopecia areata, 3-992
    Male pattern, 3-993
Baltimore College of Dental Surgery, 3-889
Bandages, 2-513
Bartholin's glands, 3-1088
Basic Life Support (BLS) procedures, 2-508
Bath, 2-575
    Sun, 2-600
Bedpan, 2-574
Bejel

See Endemic syphilis
Bell's palsy, 3-1045
Bends, the
    See Decompression sickness
Bile
    Production of by liver, 3-848

Bilharziasis
    See Flukes: Blood flukes
Biliary cirrhosis, 3-872
Bilirubin, 1-72, 2-418, 2-627
Biopsy, 1-18
Birth defects
    Congenital, 2-374
    Environmentally caused, 2-377
    German measles as cause of, 2-377
Birthmarks, 2-463, 3-993
Bites
    Animal, 2-530
    Ant, 2-533
    Human, 2-531
    Snake, 2-531
    Spider, 2-531
    Tick, 2-533
Black eye, 2-533
Black lung (coal miner's disease), 3-930
Blackheads and whiteheads
    See Acne
Blackwater fever
    See Malaria
Bladder, 3-1066
Bladder and ureter disorders
    Bladder stones (vesical calculi), 3-1078
    Cystitis (inflammation of the bladder), 3-1077
    Cystocele, 3-1080
    Interstitial cystitis, 3-1078
    Tumors, 3-1079
    Ureteral calculi (stones in ureter), 3-1076
    Ureteral stricture, 3-1076
    Urinary incontinence, 3-1076
    Urinary retention, 3-1077
Bladder stones, 3-1078
Blastomycosis, 2-739
Bleeding, 2-614
    From an injury, 2-614
    From the bladder, 2-614
    From the lungs, 2-614
    From the mouth, 2-615
    From the nose, 2-615
    From the rectum, 2-615
    From the skin, 2-615
    From the stomach, 2-615
    From the vagina, 2-614, 2-615
Bleeding, as early medical practice, 1-3
Bleeding, severe (hemorrhage), 2-614, 2-624
    What to do in event of, 2-517, 2-541

(383)

See Cardiovascular disease
Corpuscles
    See Blood cells
Cortisone, **3**-1001
Cough, **2**-453, **2**-618, **2**-648
Coughing, **3**-905
Cowper's glands, **3**-1084
CPR
    See Cardiopulmonary resuscitation
Cramps, muscle
    See Muscles, disorders of
Cretinism, **2**-423, **3**-1010
Crohn's disease (regional ileitis), **3**-859
Cross-eye (Squint), **3**-1140
    In children, **2**-469
Croup, **2**-458
Cryptococcosis (torulosis), **2**-740
CT scan
    See CAT scan
Cushing's disease
    See Cushing's syndrome
Cushing's syndrome, **3**-1007
Cutaneous leishmaniasis
    See Leishmaniasis: Oriental sore
Cuts, **2**-554
Cyanosis, **2**-619
Cystic fibrosis, **2**-461, **3**-922

D

D&C
    See Dilation and curettage
Dandruff, **3**-974
Deafness (hearing loss), **2**-620, **3**-1152 Conductive
deafness, **3**-1153
    In children, **2**-469
    In the elderly, **2**-503
    Nerve deafness, **3**-1153
Death, process of accepting
    Acceptance, **3**-1058
    Anger, **3**-1057
    Bargaining, **3**-1057
    Shock and denial, **3**-1057
Decision making
    Discrimination, **1**-102
    Judgment, **1**-103
    Self-control, **1**-103
    Willpower, **1**-103
Decompression sickness, **2**-559
Deformities
    Congenital, **2**-426
Dehydration, **1**-80
Delhi sore
    See Leishmaniasis
Delirium, **2**-558

Delirium tremens, **3**-1058
    In alcohol withdrawal, **1**-293
Delivery
    Date of, **2**-384
    Signs of, **2**-399
    See also Labor
Delivery, complications of, **2**-401
    Abnormal presentations, **2**-403
    Birth injuries, **2**-404
    Caesarean section, **2**-402
    Episiotomy, **2**-402
    False labor, **2**-401
    Forceps delivery, **2**-402
    Hemorrhage following delivery, **2**-403
    Multiple births, **2**-404
    Premature birth, **2**-401
    Premature rupture of the membranes, **2**-402
    Respiratory distress syndrome, **2**-404
    Retained placenta, **2**-403
Dementias
    Alzheimer's dementia (disease), **3**-1041
    Arteriosclerotic dementia, **3**-1041
Dengue (breakbone fever), **2**-724
Dental caries
    See Tooth disorders
Dentist
    Training of, **1**-9
Dentistry
    Endodontics, **3**-890
    History of, **3**-889, **3**-890
    Orthodontics, **3**-890
    Periodontics, **3**-890
    Prosthodontics, **3**-896
Dentures, **3**-896, **3**-897
Deoxyribonucleic acid
    See DNA
Depression, **3**-1055
    In the elderly, **2**-502
Dermatitis
    Allergic, **2**-464, **2**-678, **3**-973
    Atopic, **2**-678, **3**-971
    Atopic, in children, **2**-462
    Atopic, in infants, **2**-421
    Chronic, **3**-974
    Contact, **3**-972
    Contact, in children, **2**-470
    Dyshidrosis, **3**-974
    Irritant, **3**-972
    Nummular, **3**-975
    Seborrheic, **3**-974
    Stasis, **3**-975
    Xerotic eczema, **3**-974
DES therapy, and increased disease incidence, **3**-1109
Detached retina, **3**-1138
Diabetes, **3**-1013
    Adult-onset (type II), **1**-6, **3**-1013

As risk factor in heart disease, **3**-779
Complications of, **3**-1014
During pregnancy, **3**-1017
Juvenile onset (type I), **1**-6, **2**-475, **3**-1013
Monitoring, **3**-1018
Symptoms of, **3**-1013
Treatment of, **3**-1015
Diabetes Mellitus
See Diabetes
Diagnosis
Flow charts, **2**-641
Signs and symptoms, **2**-612
Diagnostic tests and procedures
Angiography, **1**-15
Biopsy, **1**-18
Bone marrow aspiration, **1**-18
Cardiac catheterization, **1**-16
CAT scan, **1**-15
Electrocardiography, **1**-17
Electroenchephalography, **1**-17
Electromyography, **1**-18
Endoscopes, **1**-16
MRI (magnetic resonance imaging), **1**-15
Radioactive tracers, **1**-15
Ultrasound, **1**-14
Urine analysis, **1**-19
Venipuncture (for blood analysis), **1**-18
Venography (phlebography), **1**-16
X-ray, **1**-14
Diaphragm, **3**-905
Diarrhea, **2**-620, **3**-877
Causes of, **3**-877, **3**-878
In children, **2**-460
In infants, **2**-417
Traveler's, **3**-878
Dietary fiber
Benefits of, **1**-92
Diethylstilbestrol
See DES therapy, and increased disease incidence
Diets, as supposed solution to obesity, **1**-233
See also Nutrition
Digestive system, functions of, **3**-837
Bowel movement (defecation), **3**-842
Chewing, **3**-838
Peristalsis, **3**-840
Salivation, **3**-837
Swallowing, **3**-838
Digestive system, **3**-837
Anal canal, **3**-842
Anus, **3**-842
Esophagus, **3**-838
Gallbladder, **3**-844
Large intestine, **3**-841
Lips, **3**-837
Liver, **3**-842
Mouth, **3**-837

Pancreas, **3**-844
Pharynx, **3**-837
Rectum, **3**-842
Small intestine, **3**-840
Stomach, **3**-839
Tongue, **3**-837
Digestive system, diseases of, **3**-845
Dilation and curettage, **2**-394, **3**-1105
Diphtheria, **2**-707
Discharge, mucus, **2**-620
From the colon, **2**-621
From the nose, **2**-620
From the trachea and bronchial tubes, **2**-621
Discharge, purulent, **2**-621
Disease
Causes of, **1**-29
Childhood, **2**-456
Communicable, **2**-580, **2**-703
Contagious, **2**-703
External contributors to, **2**-606
Infectious, **2**-580, **2**-703
Internal contributors to, **2**-607
Disease, predisposing factors in
Alcoholic beverages, **2**-609
Caffeine, **2**-609
Cultivated weaknesses, **2**-607
Diet, **2**-607
Drugs of abuse, **2**-609
Functional disorders, **2**-607
Hereditary weaknesses, **2**-607
Mental attitude and, **2**-609
Negative mental attitudes, **2**-609
Physical defects, **2**-607
Tobacco, **2**-609
Unhealthful habits, **2**-608
Disk
See Spinal injuries
Dislocations
See Joints, disorders of: Dislocations
Diverticulitis (diverticulosis), **3**-865
Diving emergencies, **2**-559
Decompression sickness ("the bends"), **2**-559
Dizziness, **2**-621, **3**-1051
DNA, **2**-372
Double vision (strabismus), **3**-1137
Down's syndrome (mongolism), **2**-428, **2**-468
Dressings, **2**-513
Drowning and near-drowning, **2**-558
Drug
Definition of, **1**-323
Drug abuse
Addiction, **1**-299
Charts, **1**-310, **1**-320
Factors aiding recovery from, **1**-305
Hindrances to recovery from, **1**-304
In adults, **1**-307

In teenagers, 2-493
Prevention of, 1-305
Signs of, 1-303
Treatment of, 1-304
Why the problem exists, 1-298
Drug abuse in adults
Commonly used agents, 1-307
Consequences of, 1-307
Predisposing factors, 1-307
Rehabilitation, 1-308
Drugs
Allergy to, 1-326
Idiosyncrasy to, 1-326
Illicit, 1-297
Illusionary, 1-296
Prescription, 1-328
Sensitivity to, 1-326
Stimulation of brain's reward center by, 1-296
Use of, 1-326
Drugs, illicit (drugs of abuse), 1-296
Addiction to, 1-300
Dependance on, 1-299
Tolerance for, 1-299
Drugs, over-the-counter, 1-327
Pain relievers (analgesics), 1-329
Sleep aids, 1-328
Tranquilizers, 1-333
Drugs, types of
Anti-infective agents, 1-335
Anti-inflammatory agents, 1-334
Anticancer agents, 1-336
Antiepileptic agents, 1-336
Antipsychotic agents, 1-336
Cardiovascular agents, 1-336
Diuretics, 1-336
Drugs for Parkinson's disease, 1-332
Inhalants, 1-302
Miscellaneous compounds, 1-303
Narcotic analgesics, 1-332
Narcotics, 1-300
Over-the-counter, 1-327
Prescription, 1-327
Psychoactive, 1-301
Sedatives, 1-300
Stimulants, 1-301
Dry heat applications
Electric heating pad, 2-599
Hot-water bottle, 2-599
Massage, 2-601
Progressive relaxation, 2-601
Radiant heat, 2-599
Sun bath, 2-600
Sunlamps (ultraviolet lamps), 2-600
Dry mouth (xerostomia), 3-850
DTs
See Delirium tremens

Dumdum fever
See Leishmaniasis
Dupuytren's contracture, 3-949
Dust disease
Inorganic, 3-928
Organic, 3-931
Dwarfism, 3-1006
Dysentery
See Amebic dysentery
See Bacillary dysentery
See Balantidial dysentery
Dyspepsia
See Indigestion
Dysphagia (difficulty in swallowing)
See Swallowing, difficulty in
Dyspnea, 2-616
Cardiac, 2-617
Functional hyperventilation, 2-617
Obstructive, 2-616
Of anemia, 2-617
Pulmonary, 2-617

E

Ear
External ear, 3-1142
Inner ear, 3-1142
Middle ear, 3-1142
Wax, 3-1144, 3-1145
Ear disorders (inner ear)
Labyrinthitis, 3-1152
Meniere's disease, 3-1151
Ear disorders (middle ear)
Cholesteatoma, 3-1151
Otitis media, 3-1148
Otosclerosis, 3-1150
Ear disorders (outer ear)
Ear wax, 3-1146
Foreign body, 2-544, 3-1146
Localized infection (boil, furuncle, abscess), 3-1146
Otomycosis, 3-1146
Earache, 2-650
Earplugs, 3-1145
Eating, satisfactions derived from
Gastric, 1-234
Psychic, 1-234
Visual, 1-234
Echinococcosis
See Tapeworm
Eczema
See Dermatitis
Edema, 2-622, 3-809, 3-811
Angioneurotic, 3-989
Edema, pulmonary

Fingernails, **3**-969
First aid, **2**-529
    Acute circulatory problems, **2**-541
    Allergic reactions, **2**-529
    Bites, **2**-530
    Burns, **2**-537
    Environmental overexposure, **2**-555
    Foreign bodies, **2**-544
    Fractures, **2**-548
    Medicine for, **2**-564
    Poisonings, **2**-520
    Stings, **2**-535
    Wounds and injuries, **2**-552
First-aid kits, **2**-565
Fish-skin disease
    See Ichthyosis
Fishhook, removal of from tissue, **2**-547
Fit
    See Epilepsy
Flat foot, **3**-945
Floating kidney
    See Kidneys
Fluoride, **3**-887, **3**-894
    Fluorosis, **3**-888
    In drinking water, **3**-887, **3**-894
    In toothpaste and mouthwash, **3**-888
Flu
    See Influenza
Flukes, **2**-759
    Blood flukes (schistosomiasis, bilharziasis), **2**-760
    Liver flukes, **2**-761
    Liver rot, **2**-761
    Lung flukes, **2**-761
Fluorescent lighting, **1**-72
Folliculitis, **3**-976
Fomentations, **2**-590
Fontanelles, **2**-405
Foods
    See Nutrition
Food poisoning, **2**-526
Foreign bodies
    In ear canal, **2**-544
    In eye, **2**-544
    In nose, **2**-545
    In skin, **2**-547
    In stomach, **2**-547
    In throat, **2**-545
Formula, infant, **2**-412 - **2**-415
Fractures
    See Bone fractures
Framingham health study, **1**-118
Freckles, **2**-462, **3**-987
Friedreich's ataxia, **3**-1040
Frostbite, **2**-555
Furuncles
    See Boils

G

Galen, Greek physician, **1**-323
Galenicals, **1**-323
Gallbladder, **3**-844
    Inflammation of (cholecystitis), **3**-874
Gallstones, **3**-873
Gas (flatulence), **3**-876
Gas (belching), **3**-876
Gastritis, **3**-854
Gastroenteritis, **2**-714
Genes, **2**-372
German measles, **2**-472, **2**-727
    As cause of birth defects, **2**-377
Giardiasis, **2**-747
Gigantism, **3**-1006
Gingivitis, **3**-886, **3**-895
Gingivitis, acute ulcerative
    See Trench mouth
Glaucoma, **3**-1134
    Acute (closed-angle), **3**-1135
    Chronic (open-angle), **3**-1135
    Congenital, **2**-469, **3**-1135
Glomeruli, **3**-1068
Goiter, **3**-1009
Gonorrhea, **3**-1115
Graves' disease, **3**-1009
Grief
    Acute mourning, **3**-1057
    Denial, **3**-1057
    Resolution or reorganization, **3**-1057
    Shock, **3**-1057
Ground itch
    See Hookworms
Growing pains, **2**-453
Guinea worms, **2**-759
Gums (gingiva), **3**-886
    Gingivitis, **3**-886, **3**-895
    Periodontitis, **3**-895

H

Hair, **3**-969
    Gray, **3**-993
    Washing of home patient's, **2**-577
Hair disorders
    Hair loss (alopecia, baldness), **3**-992
Halitosis, **2**-629
Hangnail, **3**-992
Hansen's disease
    See Leprosy
Harelip (cleft lip), **3**-845
Hashimoto's disease, **3**-1010
Hay fever, **2**-676, **2**-679, **3**-910
    In children, **2**-470

Headache, **2**-622, **2**-658, **3**-1050
    Migraine, **3**-1051
    Tension, **3**-1050
    Vascular, **3**-1051
Headaches
    In children, **2**-454
Health
    Definition of, **1**-23, **1**-31
    Lifestyle in relation to, **1**-30, **1**-124
    Mental, **1**-99
    Spiritual, **1**-112
Health habits
    Good and bad, chart of, **1**-120
Health studies
    Adventist health studies, **1**-121
    Breslow's study, **1**-119
    The Framingham study, **1**-118
Health-care professionals
    Types of, **1**-8
Hearing aids, **3**-1154
Hearing loss
    See Deafness (hearing loss)
Hearing, mechanism of, **3**-1143
Heart, **3**-767
    A-V node, **3**-768
    Atria, **3**-767
    Bundle of His, **3**-768
    Coronary arteries, **3**-768
    Heart sounds, **3**-769
    Heartbeat, **3**-769
    Pacemaker, **3**-768
    Size, **3**-767
    Valves, **3**-768
    Ventricles, **3**-767
    Weight, **3**-767
Heart attack, **3**-781, **3**-783
    Infarct, **3**-783
    Prevention of, **3**-788
    Recovering from (rehabilitation), **3**-788
    Symptoms of, **3**-783
    What to do in event of, **2**-541, **3**-784
Heart disease
    See Cardiovascular disease, Atherosclerosis
Heart rhythms (rate), **3**-790
    Atrial fibrillation, **3**-791
    Atrial flutter, **3**-791
    Heart block, **3**-792
    Pacemakers as regulators of, **3**-792
    Palpitation, **2**-631, **3**-790
    Tachycardia, **3**-790
    Ventricular fibrillation, **3**-792
    Ventricular tachycardia, **3**-792
Heart valve disease, **3**-793
    Aortic incompetence, **3**-795
    Aortic stenosis, **3**-794
    Mitral incompetence, **3**-794
    Mitral stenosis, **3**-793
    Pulmonary stenosis and incompetence, **3**-795
    Tricuspid stenosis and incompetence, **3**-795
Heart valves, **3**-793
    Aortic, **3**-793
    Mitral, **3**-793
    Pulmonary, **3**-793
    Tricuspid, **3**-793
Heartburn, **2**-625, **3**-851
Heat, effects of, **2**-587
Heat cramps, **2**-556, **2**-623
Heat exhaustion (heat prostration), **2**-556, **2**-623
Heatstroke (sunstroke), **2**-556, **2**-623
Heimlich manuever, **2**-546
Hemangioma
    See Birthmarks
Hematoma
    In subdural hemorrhage, **3**-1034
Hemiplegia, **3**-1038
Hemophilia
    See Blood, diseases of
Hemorrhage
    See Bleeding, severe
Hemorrhoids, **3**-868
    See Veins, diseases of
Hepatitis, **3**-869
    Chronic active, **3**-871
    In children, **2**-461
    In teenagers, **2**-493
    Non-A, Non-B (post-transfusion), **3**-871
    Type A (infectious), **3**-870
    Type B (serum), **3**-870
Herbs, medicinal, **1**-337
    In relation to drug extract of, **1**-339
Heredity
    As risk factor in heart disease, **3**-779
    Versus environment, as influence on child, **2**-374
Hernia, **2**-624, **3**-862
    First aid for, **2**-560
    Hiatus, **3**-853
    In children, **2**-461
    Intestinal, **3**-862
    Umbilical, **2**-419
Herniated disk, **3**-951
Herpangina, **2**-459
Herpes
    Facial herpes, **3**-979
    Genital, **3**-1120
    Herpes Simplex Type I, **3**-979
    Herpes Simplex Type II, **3**-1120
    Primary, **3**-979
    Recurrent, **3**-979
    Zoster (shingles), **3**-980
Herpes simplex virus
    See Cold sores, Fever blisters
Hiatus hernia

L

Labor
    "Breaking of the bag of waters," **2**-399
    "Show," **2**-399
    False labor, **2**-401
    First stage, **2**-399
    Second stage, **2**-400
    Signs of, **2**-399
    Third stage, **2**-400
Lactose intolerance, **2**-454, **3**-858
    In teenagers, **2**-493
Large intestine, **3**-841
    Appendix, **3**-841
    Ascending colon, **3**-841
    Cecum, **3**-841
    Descending colon, **3**-841
    Sigmoid colon, **3**-841
    Transverse colon, **3**-841
Larynx, **3**-901
Larynx, diseases of, **3**-914
    Hoarseness, **3**-915
    Laryngitis, **3**-915
    Vocal cord damage, **3**-915
Leishmaniasis
    Espundia (American leishmaniasis), **2**-747
    Kala-azar (dumdum fever), **2**-748
    Oriental sore (tropical sore, Delhi sore), **2**-747
Lens, disorders of
    Aging eyes (presbyopia), **3**-1137
    Astigmatism, **3**-1137
    Blindness, **3**-1138
    Cataract, **3**-1136
    Double vision, **3**-1137
    Farsightedness, **3**-1137
    Nearsightedness, **3**-1136
    Refractive errors, **3**-1136
Leprosy (Hansen's disease), **2**-708
    Lepromatous leprosy, **2**-709
    Tuberculoid leprosy, **2**-709
Leptospirosis, **2**-721
Leukemia, **2**-682, **3**-823 - **3**-825
    Acute, **3**-824
    See also Blood, diseases of
    Chronic, **3**-825
    Granulocytic, **3**-824
    Lymphocytic, **3**-824
Leukoplakia, **3**-850, **3**-916
Lice
    Body, **3**-982
    Head, **3**-982
    In children, **2**-464
    Pubic (crab), **3**-982
Life
    Defined, **1**-23
    Relation of health to, **1**-23

(398)

Life expectancy, **1**-24
Life, dimensions of
    Breadth (quality), **1**-26
    Depth (love for God and man), **1**-27
    Length, **1**-25
    Length (life expectancy), **1**-24
Lifestyle
    As consideration in establishing a home, **2**-365
    Healthful, **1**-124, **1**-125
    Influence of on health and disease, **1**-117
    Westerner's, **1**-124
Lifestyle diseases, **1**-8, **1**-29
Lipids, blood
    See Cholesterol
Lipoproteins, **3**-777
Lips
    Cracking of (cheilosis), **3**-846
Lister, Dr. Joseph
    Control of wound infection pioneered by, **1**-5
Little's disease
    See Cerebral palsy
Liver, **3**-842
    Abscess of, **3**-873
    Cancer of, **3**-873
    Cirrhosis of, **3**-871
    Functions of, **3**-843
Liver rot
    See Flukes
Liver spots, **3**-987
Lobar pneumonia
    See Pneumonia
Lockjaw
    See Tetanus
Louse typhus
    See Typhus
Low blood pressure, **3**-804
Low blood sugar
    See Hypoglycemia
LSD (Iysergic acid diethylamide), **1**-302
Lump in the throat, **2**-628
Lumpy Jaw
    See Actinomycosis
"Lumpy breasts," **1**-262, **2**-616
Lung abscess, **3**-927
Lungs, **3**-902
    Covering of (pleura), **3**-905
Lupus (SLE), **3**-957
Lyme disease, **2**-720
Lymph, **3**-826
Lymph nodes
    Infection-fighting role of, **3**-827, **3**-828
    Lymphocytes, **3**-827
    Phagocytes, **3**-827
    Swollen (lymphadenopathy), **3**-831
Lymphatic system, **3**-826
    Lymph nodes, **3**-826

Selective Atlas of Normal Anatomy

Special acknowledgment is due Lederle Laboratories for the series of color plates appearing in the section "Selective Atlas of Normal Anatomy," these being part of a larger series of paintings by Paul Peck, copyrighted by Lederle Laboratories Division, American Cyanamid Company, Pearl River, N.Y., and included in this volume by permission.

Anatomy of the Heart

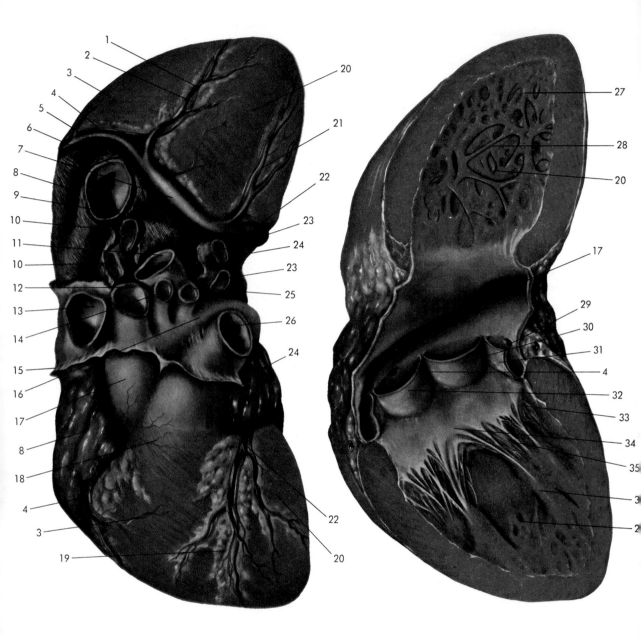

1 Middle cardiac vein	13 Superior vena cava	25 Left subclavian artery
2 Posterior descending branch of right coronary artery	14 Left common carotid artery	26 Left branch of pulmonary artery
	15 Pericardium	27 Trabeculae carneae
3 Right ventricle	16 Aortic arch	28 Trabecula tendinea
4 Right coronary artery	17 Ascending aorta	29 Left coronary artery
5 Small cardiac vein	18 Conus arteriosus	30 Posterior semilunar valve
6 Inferior vena cava	19 Anterior descending branch of left coronary artery	31 Left semilunar valve
7 Coronary sinus		32 Right semilunar valve
8 Right auricle	20 Left ventricle	33 Posterior cusp of mitral (bicuspid) valve
9 Left atrium	21 Posterior vein of left ventricle	34 Anterior cusp of mitral (bicuspid) valve
10 Right pulmonary vein	22 Great cardiac vein	35 Chordae tendineae
11 Right branch of pulmonary artery	23 Left pulmonary vein	36 Papillary muscle
12 Innominate artery	24 Left auricle	

Anatomy of the Stomach

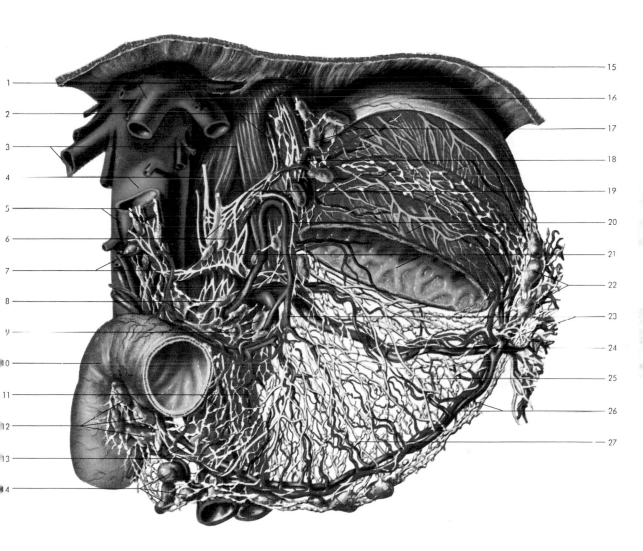

1 Middle and left hepatic veins
2 Right vagus nerve and esophagus
3 Right hepatic vein and crura of diaphragm
4 Inferior vena cava and greater splanchnic nerve
5 Portal vein and hepatic artery
6 Celiac plexus and celiac artery
7 Hepatic lymph node and hepatic rami of vagus nerve
8 Gastroduodenal artery and suprapyloric lymph nodes

9 Superior gastric lymph nodes
10 Duodenum
11 Superior mesenteric artery and vein
12 Subpyloric lymph nodes
13 Right gastroepiploic artery and vein
14 Inferior gastric lymph nodes
15 Diaphragm
16 Serosa
17 Paracardial lymph nodes
18 Left vagus nerve and longitudinal muscular layer

19 Abdominal aorta and circular muscular layer
20 Left gastric artery and oblique muscular layer
21 Celiac rami of vagus nerve and gastric mucosa
22 Splenic lymph nodes
23 Left gastric (coronary) vein and splenic rami of vagus nerve
24 Splenic artery and vein
25 Gastric rami of vagus nerve
26 Left gastroepiploic artery and vein
27 Gastric lymphatic plexus

The Sympathetic Nervous System

ABDOMINAL PORTION

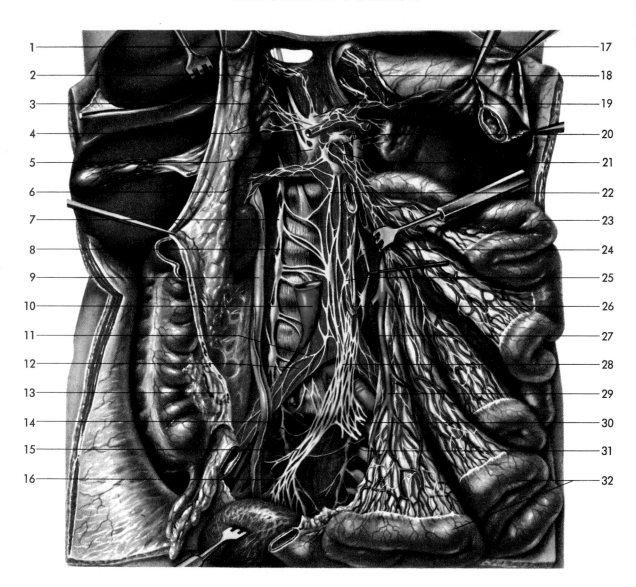

1 Phrenic ganglion and plexus
2 Greater splanchnic nerve
3 Lesser splanchnic nerve
4 Suprarenal plexus
5 Aorticorenal ganglion
6 Right renal artery and plexus
7 Right lumbar sympathetic ganglion
8 Right sympathetic trunk
9 Ureter
10 Vena cava
11 Iliac plexus

12 Right common iliac artery
13 Mesocolon (cut)
14 Right sacral sympathetic ganglion
15 Right pelvic plexus
16 Pudendal plexus
17 Left vagus nerve
18 Right vagus nerve
19 Celiac plexus and right celiac ganglion
20 Superior mesenteric ganglion and plexus
21 Left celiac ganglion; superior mesenteric artery

22 Abdominal aortic plexus
23 Jejunum
24 Left lumbar sympathetic ganglion
25 Inferior mesenteric ganglion
26 Inferior mesenteric plexus
27 Left sympathetic trunk
28 Hypogastric plexus
29 Branches of superior mesenteric artery and vein
30 Left pelvic plexus
31 Left sacral sympathetic ganglion
32 Ileum

The Sympathetic Nervous System

CEPHALIC, CERVICAL AND THORACIC PORTIONS

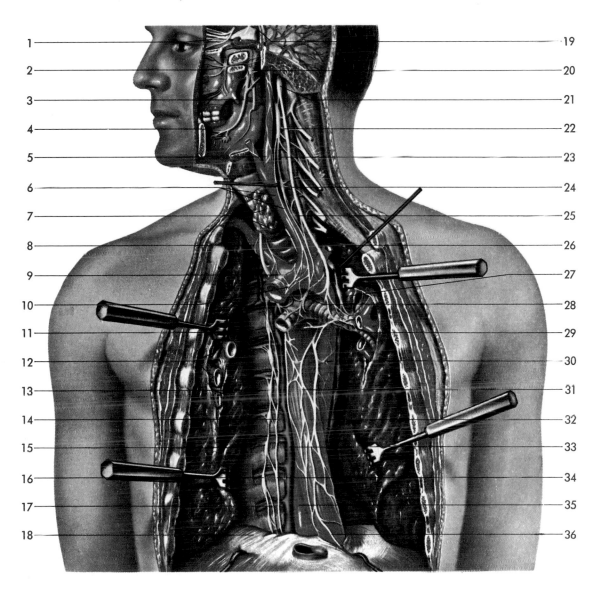

1 Ciliary ganglion
2 Sphenopalatine ganglion
3 Lingual nerve
4 Submandibular ganglion
5 Internal carotid artery
6 Common carotid artery; superior cardiac nerve
7 Thyroid gland; recurrent laryngeal nerve
8 Right vagus nerve
9 Aortic arch
10 Superficial cardiac plexus
11 Fifth thoracic sympathetic ganglion

12 Pulmonary artery and vein
13 Seventh thoracic sympathetic ganglion
14 Greater splanchnic nerve
15 Intercostal artery, vein and nerve
16 Tenth thoracic sympathetic ganglion
17 Lesser splanchnic nerve
18 Diaphragm
19 Trigeminal nerve
20 Otic ganglion
21 Nodose ganglion
22 Superior cervical sympathetic ganglion
23 Cervical sympathetic trunk
24 Middle cervical sympathetic ganglion

25 Inferior cervical sympathetic ganglion
26 Left vagus nerve
27 Fourth thoracic sympathetic ganglion
28 Cardiac ganglion
29 Anterior pulmonary plexus
30 Aortic plexus
31 Esophageal plexus
32 Esophagus
33 Azygos vein
34 Splanchnic ganglion
35 Aorta
36 Anterior gastric cord of vagus

The Coronary Arteries

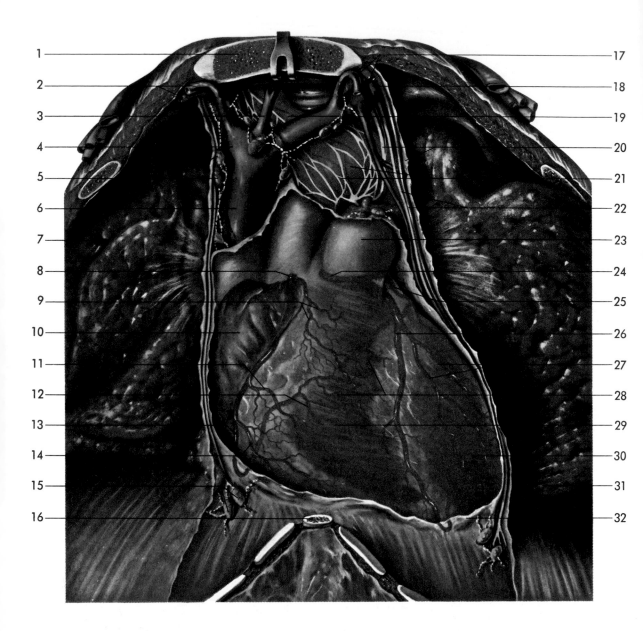

1 Manubrium
2 Right internal mammary artery and vein
3 Thyreoidea ima vein
4 Right brachiocephalic vein
5 Anterior superior mediastinal lymph nodes
6 Superior vena cava
7 Right lung
8 Right coronary artery
9 Preventricular arteries
10 Right atrium
11 Lateral branch of right coronary artery

12 Posterior descending branch of right circumflex artery
13 Right circumflex artery
14 Right marginal artery
15 Anterior inferior mediastinal lymph nodes
16 Xiphoid process
17 Left internal mammary artery and vein
18 Left brachiocephalic vein
19 Brachiocephalic trunk
20 Vagus nerve; mediastinal pleura (Cut)
21 Superficial cardiac plexus; arch of aorta

22 Pericardiacophrenic artery; phrenic nerve
23 Pulmonary artery
24 Left coronary artery
25 Left circumflex artery
26 Anterior descending branch of left coronary artery
27 Left marginal arteries
28 Left ventricular branches
29 Right ventricle
30 Left ventricle
31 Left lung
32 Pericardium (cut)

Anatomy of the Ear

FRONTAL SECTION SHOWING COMPONENT PARTS OF THE HUMAN EAR

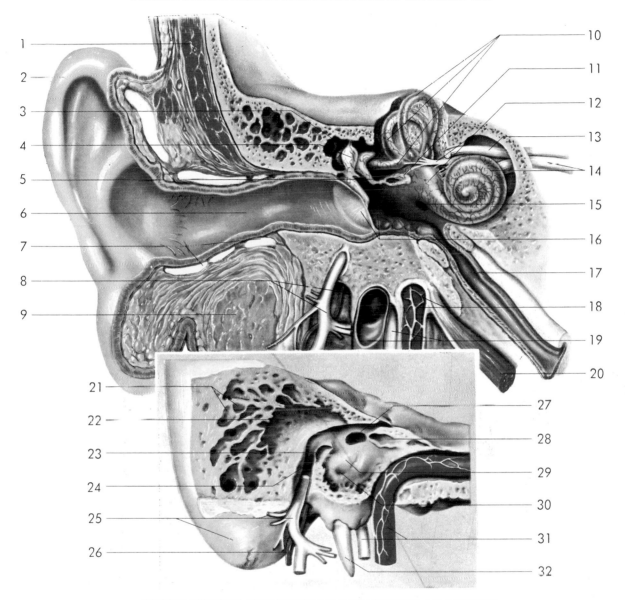

SECTION THROUGH RIGHT TEMPORAL BONE SHOWING RELATIONSHIP BETWEEN MASTOID CELLS AND TYMPANIC CAVITY

1 Temporal muscle
2 Helix
3 Epitympanic recess
4 Malleus
5 Incus
6 External acoustic meatus
7 Cartilaginous part of external acoustic meatus
8 Facial nerve and stylomastoid artery
9 Parotid gland
10 Semicircular canals
11 Stapes
12 Vestibule and vestibular nerve

13 Facial nerve
14 Cochlea and cochlear nerve
15 Cochlear (round) window
16 Tympanic membrane and tympanic cavity
17 Auditory (Eustachian) tube
18 Internal carotid artery and sympathetic nerve plexus
19 Glossopharyngeal nerve and internal jugular vein
20 Levator veli palatini muscle
21 Mastoid cells
22 Tympanic antrum

23 Cavity of the pyramidal eminence for the stapedius
24 Facial canal
25 Facial nerve and mastoid process
26 Stylomastoid artery
27 Vestibular (oval) window
28 Cochleariform process
29 Promontory
30 Cochlear fenestra
31 Internal carotid artery and glossopharyngeal nerve
32 Styloid process

Region of the Mouth

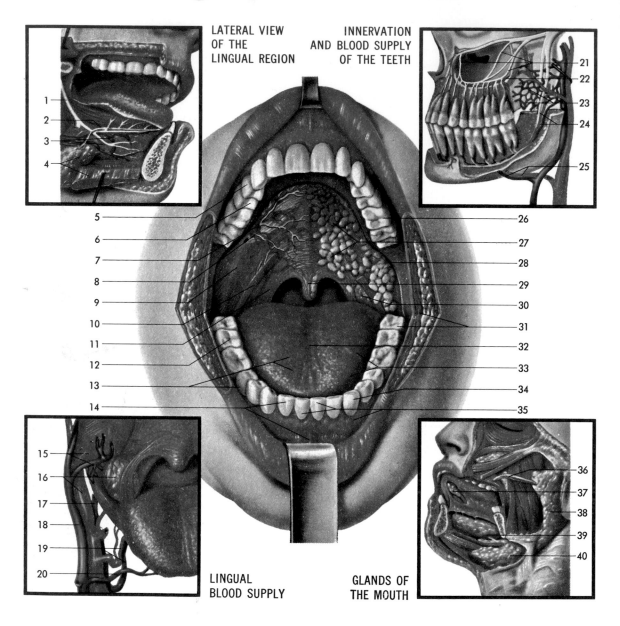

LATERAL VIEW OF THE LINGUAL REGION

INNERVATION AND BLOOD SUPPLY OF THE TEETH

LINGUAL BLOOD SUPPLY

GLANDS OF THE MOUTH

1 Lingual nerve
2 Submaxillary duct
3 Sublingual branches of lingual artery and vein
4 Submaxillary gland; mylohyoid muscle
5 First premolar
6 Second premolar
7 Greater palatine artery and nerve
8 Lesser palatine artery and nerve
9 Pterygomandibular raphe
10 Glossopalatine muscle
11 Pharyngopalatinus muscle
12 Second molar
13 Filiform papillae; second premolar
14 Lateral incisor; frenulum of lower lip

15 Internal maxillary artery and vein
16 External carotid artery; palatine tonsil
17 Internal jugular vein
18 Posterior facial vein
19 Lingual artery and vein
20 Ranine vein
21 Anterior, middle and posterior superior alveolar nerves
22 Posterior superior alveolar artery
23 Pterygoid venous plexus
24 Inferior alveolar nerve and artery
25 External maxillary artery; anterior facial vein
26 First molar
27 Palatine glands

28 Cut edge of mucous membrane
29 Uvula
30 Palatine tonsils
31 Third molar; buccinator muscle
32 Median sulcus of tongue
33 Fungiform papillae
34 Canine
35 Central incisors; gingiva
36 Parotid duct
37 Anterior lingual gland
38 Parotid gland
39 Sublingual gland
40 Submaxillary gland

Anatomy of the Lung

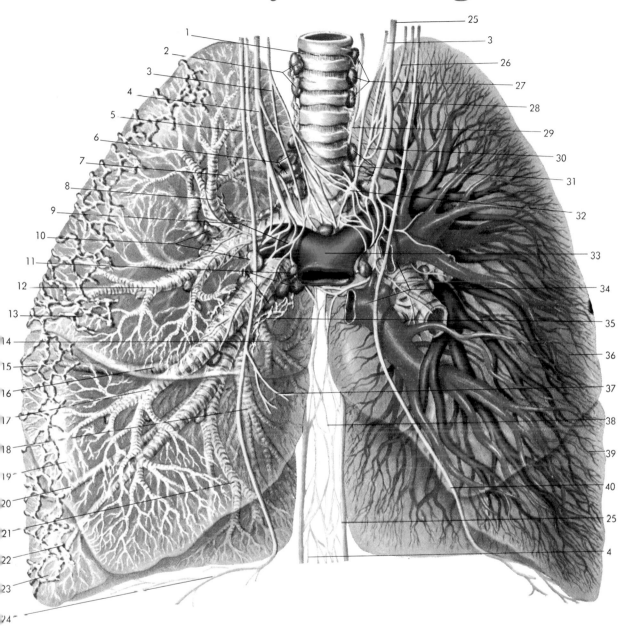

1 Trachea
2 Right tracheal lymph nodes
3 Superior cardiac nerve
4 Right vagus nerve
5 Right phrenic nerve
6 Right superior tracheobronchial lymph nodes
7 Posterior bronchial branch, upper lobe
8 Apical bronchial branch, upper lobe
9 Anterior pulmonary plexus
10 Interbronchial lymph nodes
11 Inferior tracheobronchial lymph nodes
12 Anterior bronchial branch, upper lobe
13 Upper lobe of right lung
14 Superior bronchial branch, lower lobe

15 Superficial lymphatic plexus
16 Lateral bronchial branch, middle lobe
17 Medial bronchial branch, middle lobe
18 Posterior basal bronchial branch, lower lobe
19 Middle lobe of right lung
20 Lateral basal bronchial branch, lower lobe
21 Medial basal bronchial branch, lower lobe
22 Anterior basal bronchial branch, lower lobe
23 Lower lobe of right lung
24 Phrenicoabdominal branch of phrenic nerve
25 Left vagus nerve
26 Middle cardiac nerve

27 Left tracheal lymph nodes
28 Inferior cardiac nerve
29 Recurrent laryngeal nerve
30 Superficial cardiac plexus
31 Left superior tracheobronchial lymph nodes
32 Inferior cardiac ganglion
33 Pulmonary artery
34 Left pulmonary veins
35 Deep lymphatic plexus
36 Upper lobe of left lung
37 Pericardial branch of phrenic nerve
38 Esophageal plexus
39 Lower lobe of left lung
40 Left phrenic nerve

The Intervertebral Disks

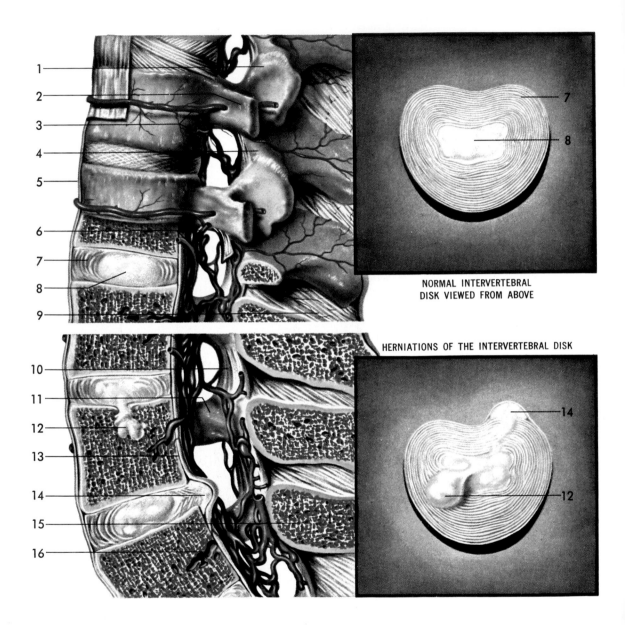

NORMAL INTERVERTEBRAL
DISK VIEWED FROM ABOVE

HERNIATIONS OF THE INTERVERTEBRAL DISK

1 Superior articular process
2 Transverse process
3 Lumbar artery and vein
4 Inferior articular process
5 Anterior longitudinal ligament
6 Internal vertebral venous plexus

7 Fibrous ring of intervertebral disk
8 Nucleus pulposus
9 Interspinous ligament
10 Ligamentum flavum
11 Lamina
12 Herniation of nucleus pulposus into
   the spongiosa (Schmorl lesion)

13 Posterior longitudinal ligament
14 Herniation of nucleus pulposus beneath
   the posterior longitudinal ligament
15 Spinous process
16 Basivertebral vein

Anatomy of the Brain

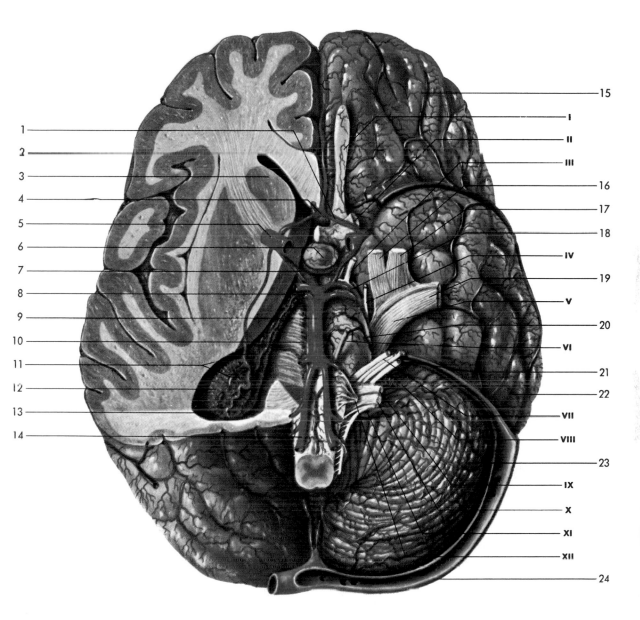

Anatomy of the Ankle

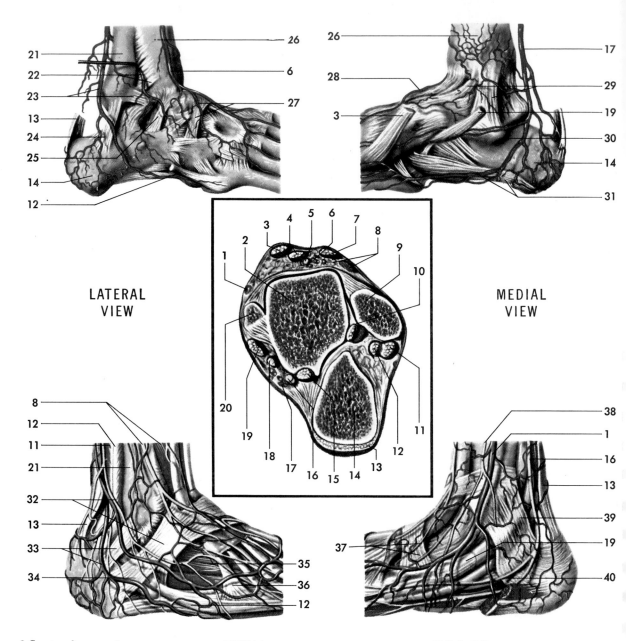

LATERAL
VIEW

MEDIAL
VIEW

1 Great saphenous vein
2 Talus
3 Tendon of tibialis anterior
4 Tendon of extensor hallucis longus
5 Deep peroneal nerve
6 Anterior tibial artery
7 Tendon of extensor digitorum longus
8 Peroneus tertius muscle and superficial peroneal nerve
9 Lateral malleolus
10 Posterior talofibular ligament
11 Tendon of peroneus longus
12 Tendon of peroneus brevis
13 Calcaneal tendon
14 Calcaneus
15 Tendon of flexor hallucis longus

16 Tibial nerve
17 Posterior tibial artery
18 Tendon of flexor digitorum longus
19 Tendon of tibialis posterior
20 Medial malleolus
21 Fibula
22 Perforating peroneal artery and anterior ligament of external malleolus
23 Peroneal artery and anterior talofibular ligament
24 Calcaneofibular ligament
25 External talocalcaneal ligament
26 Tibia
27 Lateral tarsal artery and dorsal cuboideo-navicular ligament
28 Dorsal pedis artery

29 Deltoid ligament
30 Sustentaculum tali
31 Long plantar ligament and lateral plantar artery
32 Sural nerve and cruciate ligament
33 Superior peroneal retinaculum and small saphenous vein
34 Inferior peroneal retinaculum
35 Extensor digitorum brevis muscle
36 Tendon of peroneus tertius
37 Medial dorsal cutaneous nerve and cruciate ligament
38 Saphenous nerve
39 Laciniate ligament
40 Medial plantar nerve

Pelvis and Hip Joint

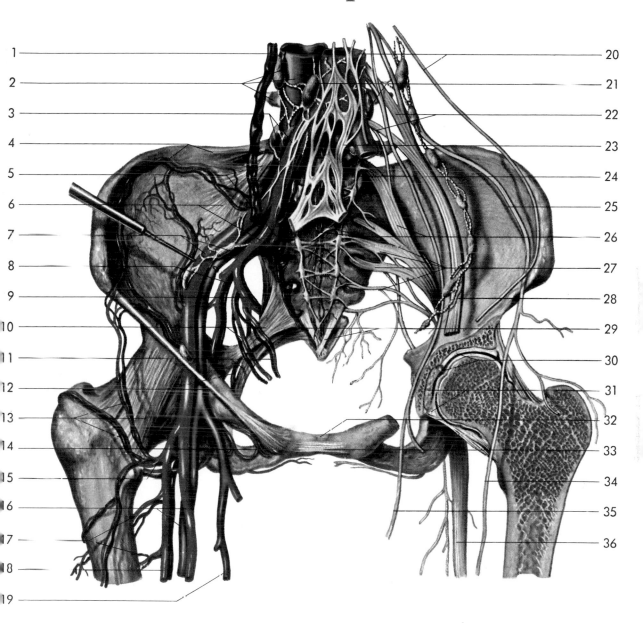

1 — 20
2 — 21
3 — 22
4 — 23
5 — 24
6 — 25
7 — 26
8 — 27
9 — 28
10 — 29
11 — 30
12 — 31
13 — 32
14 — 33
15 — 34
16 — 35
17 — 36
18
19

1 Ovarian artery and vein
2 Vena cava; lumbar lymph nodes
3 Right common iliac artery and vein
4 Iliolumbar ligament; branches of iliolumbar artery and vein
5 Lumbosacral ligament; superior gluteal artery and vein
6 Anterior sacroiliac ligament; internal iliac (hypogastric) artery
7 External iliac artery and vein
8 Obturator artery and vein
9 Inferior gluteal artery and vein
10 Sacrospinous ligament; uterine artery and vein
11 Sacrotuberous ligament; vaginal artery and vein

12 Inguinal ligament; internal pudendal artery
13 Iliofemoral ligament; branches of lateral femoral circumflex artery and vein
14 Lacunar ligament
15 Lateral femoral circumflex artery and vein
16 Femoral artery and vein
17 Perforating arteries and veins
18 Deep femoral artery and vein
19 Great saphenous vein
20 Aorta; ilioinguinal nerve
21 Lateral aortic lymph nodes
22 Lumbar nerves
23 Hypogastric sympathetic plexus
24 Sympathetic trunk

25 Lateral femoral cutaneous nerve
26 Middle sacral artery and vein; lumbosacral trunk
27 Sacral nerves
28 Femoral nerve
29 Lateral sacral artery and vein; anterior sacrococcygeal ligament
30 Lunate articular cartilage; joint cavity
31 Acetabular fat pad; ligamentum teres
32 Interpubic fibrocartilage
33 Superior pubic ligament
34 Anterior branch of lateral femoral cutaneous nerve
35 Obturator nerve
36 Great sciatic nerve

Anatomy of the Hand

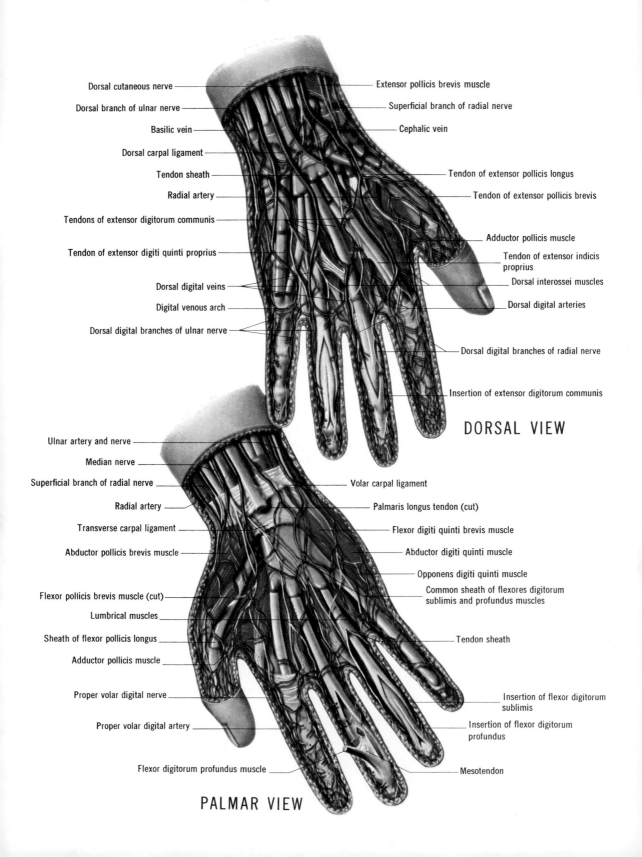

Dorsal cutaneous nerve

Dorsal branch of ulnar nerve

Basilic vein

Dorsal carpal ligament

Tendon sheath

Radial artery

Tendons of extensor digitorum communis

Tendon of extensor digiti quinti proprius

Dorsal digital veins

Digital venous arch

Dorsal digital branches of ulnar nerve

Extensor pollicis brevis muscle

Superficial branch of radial nerve

Cephalic vein

Tendon of extensor pollicis longus

Tendon of extensor pollicis brevis

Adductor pollicis muscle

Tendon of extensor indicis proprius

Dorsal interossei muscles

Dorsal digital arteries

Dorsal digital branches of radial nerve

Insertion of extensor digitorum communis

DORSAL VIEW

Ulnar artery and nerve

Median nerve

Superficial branch of radial nerve

Radial artery

Transverse carpal ligament

Abductor pollicis brevis muscle

Flexor pollicis brevis muscle (cut)

Lumbrical muscles

Sheath of flexor pollicis longus

Adductor pollicis muscle

Proper volar digital nerve

Proper volar digital artery

Flexor digitorum profundus muscle

Volar carpal ligament

Palmaris longus tendon (cut)

Flexor digiti quinti brevis muscle

Abductor digiti quinti muscle

Opponens digiti quinti muscle

Common sheath of flexores digitorum sublimis and profundus muscles

Tendon sheath

Insertion of flexor digitorum sublimis

Insertion of flexor digitorum profundus

Mesotendon

PALMAR VIEW